*Solidarity and Treason*

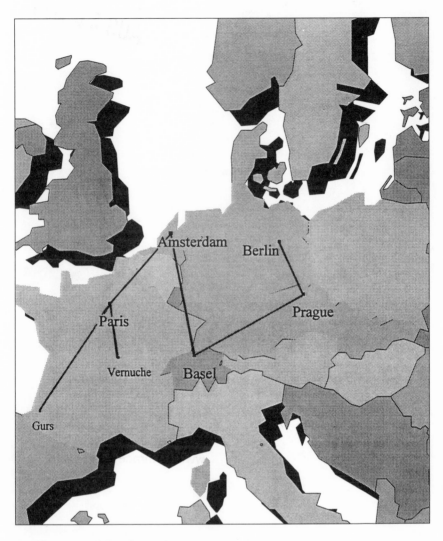

*Our European exile lasted more than seven years.*

# SOLIDARITY

## *a n d*

# TREASON

*Resistance and Exile, 1933-1940*

# LISA FITTKO

*Translated by Roslyn Theobald*
*in collaboration with the author*

Northwestern University Press
Evanston, Illinois

Northwestern University Press
Evanston, Illinois 60208-4210

First published as *Solidarität Unerwünscht: Meine Flucht durch Europa, Erinnerungen 1933-1940*. Copyright © 1992 by Carl Hanser Verlag. English translation published 1993 by arrangement with Carl Hanser Verlag. Copyright © 1993 by Northwestern University Press. All rights reserved.
First paperback printing, 1995
Printed in the United States of America

**Library of Congress Cataloging-in-Publication Data**

Fittko, Lisa, 1909–
    [Solidarität unerwünscht. English]
    Solidarity and treason : resistance and exile, 1933–40 / Lisa Fittko ; translated by Roslyn Theobald in collaboration with the author.
        p. cm.
    ISBN 0-8101-1129-2.  ISBN 0-8101-1130-6 (pbk.)
    1. Fittko, Lisa, 1909– .  2. Anti-Nazi movement—Germany—Berlin—Biography.  3. Political refugees—Germany—History—20th century.  4. National socialism—German—Berlin.  5. Germans—Czechoslovakia—History—20th century.  6. Germans—France—History—20th century.  7. Holocaust, Jewish (1939-1945)  8. Germany—Politics and government—1933-1945.  I. Title.
DD256.4.B47F58413      1993
943.086'092—dc 20
[B]                                                          93-38564
                                                              CIP

The paper used in this publication meets the minimum requirements of the American National Standard for Information Sciences—Permanence of Paper for Printed Library Materials, ANSI Z39.48-1984.

# Contents

# JANUARY 30, 1933

## THE TORCHLIGHT PARADE

I heard the commotion as I got off the elevated train at Halle Gate. Then I saw the mass of brown uniforms standing around on the square.

I had known since noon when the call came into Hilde's office: "Hitler's become Chancellor!" Later, as I crossed Alexanderplatz, I saw storm troopers gathering. But here, in our district—in the middle of Kreuzberg? Already confident enough to show themselves out in the open, in public!

As alarming as Hilde's call was, it was not really a bolt out of the blue, and from the very beginning this Monday had hardly been an ordinary day. We were waiting: something is going to happen today; they'll decide today.

Then it did happen, and we got our decision. Hindenburg asked Hitler to name a cabinet. It was clear that beginning on this day fascism would rule openly in Germany. We had been prepared for it, we had seen the danger clearly, everything had pointed toward this outcome. Just yesterday, in the Lustgarten, along with a hundred thousand other Berliners, we had demonstrated against the growing threat of fascism. But we hadn't imagined a "national revolution" like this. Now it was here, and it was legal. Through the good graces of Hindenburg.

"*Sieg Heil! Sieg Heil!*," the Brownshirts yelled. I looked at people who, having left work at the usual time of day, were rushing home. Some of them looked around, some hesitated, their jackets and coats pulled more tightly around them in the January air. Many walked faster than usual. Were we simply bystanders, observing events? A few looked away and started walking in another direction. Something was not right, I could see

1

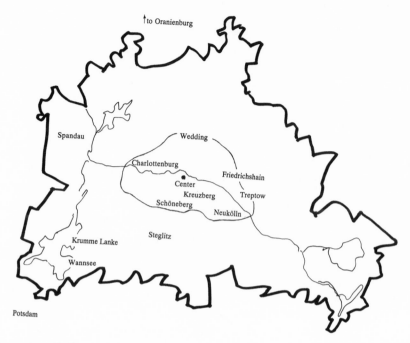

*Metropolitan Berlin*

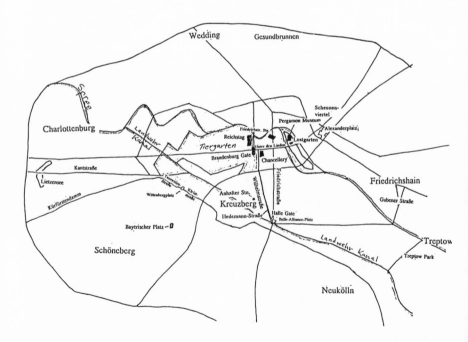

*Central Berlin*

it, but this just could not be true. A demonstration without police presence was unthinkable.

In order to get a good look at everything, I leaned up against a wall as if I were waiting for someone. Aha! there they were, the police, three armored cars; there they sat, their rifles held between their knees, helmets strapped on. But not the way they usually were at demonstrations, in the middle of things; this time they kept their distance and could hardly be seen through the trees. There they were, our Prussian police. Policing whom? Eight days ago they had stood on the rooftops with their machine guns protecting the Nazis from the populace on Bülow and Alexanderplatz.—I've got to get out of here, home! I turned and walked away toward Belle-Alliance Square.

When I came to the little café where a few of our chess players could always be found, I stopped and thought for a moment, and then went down the steps to see who was there; I needed to talk to someone. Considering the time of day, there were more people in the back room than usual; the chessboards were there as always, people were sitting at tables, but no one seemed to be playing. Kurt was there, and Else, Walter, Erich, and a few others—I can no longer remember all of their names. Yes, of course they had seen what was happening out there. And what else could we expect? Military dictatorship? Nonsense. We've already got it. Storm trooper terrorism, that was certain. We've got that too. But—until now we had always been able to defend ourselves. And now? Many of us would have to disappear. Take cover, yes, but we would not disappear. Never. The struggle against fascism had to continue, especially now. Underground.

But how? What could we do? The two left-wing parties . . . forming a united front after all? Look, you don't even believe that yourself . . . it just won't happen. Can't wait for miracles, time to take action. Of course we'll have to do a flyer, hand it out here in Kreuzberg, in the factories, too. First thing tomorrow. Where's the mimeograph machine? Erwin has it. We'll write the text now, tonight! But first we should find out what's going to happen at the torchlight parade. And the attacks on working-class bars.

"I'll go take a look," I said. I had to see for myself. "We'll meet here afterwards."

"All right. They don't know this place."

I left a little later. I had decided I didn't need to see the parade itself; instead I went directly to Wilhelmstrasse where I could see the demonstrators assembling.

The square in front of the Chancellery filled up quickly. From a distance you could hear the shouting, the noise, and the bands, and you could hear marching boots—the murderers were marching and the crowds cheered them on. I'm at the front. I slowly push my way toward the Chancellery; I want to see and hear everything. The crowd is growing, people packed together. And the storm troopers are marching down Wilhelmstrasse. In the flickering light of torches I see only the shadows of hanging banners. I hear boots. And I hear their song:

*Volk ans Gewehr! Volk ans Gewehr!*

"Countrymen, to arms!" Blaring out into the streets. The menacing roll of the drums, nearer and nearer. The cheering masses. They're cheering the menace on. Don't they know what that menace means to them?

I want to understand this pandemonium. I'd seen this kind of thing before, once when I was passing by the Sports Stadium during a Nazi rally, but I didn't understand it. The enthusiasm for terror, for murder, for everything we hate. Of course, I know: economic crisis, unemployment, Nazi demagoguery—still, I just can't comprehend it. All around me, shining eyes, screaming voices, pandemonium. But maybe, just maybe, not everyone has come here to yell along with the crowd; maybe there are a few like me who've simply come to take a look for themselves. I see some inquisitive faces! We are, after all, in Berlin!

Marching feet, beating drums. For a moment everything is still. I know what will come next. In my pockets my hands are closing into fists.

*Die Fahnen hoch, die Reihen fest geschlossen!*
*SA marschiert . . .*

"Raise the banners," the murderous ranks are closed. People are yelling, cheering, and singing, paying homage to the pimp Horst Wessel; he'd been blasted away by his professional colleague, and now the Nazis were making him their national hero.

Heads are turned toward the Chancellery. Something's happening on the third floor. I crane my neck to see. The "venerable field marshal" is coming to the window. The man who was elected to protect us from Hitler. Wild ovations. I can see another figure behind him—it's Meissner, minister of state. And now I see the "Führer"; his arm is raised and he's swinging it

around as though he were in a trance. Deafening roar: *Sieg Heil! Heil Hitler!*
The crowd is closing in. A voice shouts, "Hey you, where's your arm?"

Another voice: "I saw that too! And her mouth is frozen shut."

"Hey, is something wrong with you?"

How can I be so stupid? What *is* wrong with me? Never occurred to me that everyone here would be a follower. That anyone would take any notice of me at all. How am I going to get out of here? I'm so wedged in I can't even move. The man who first started harassing me is yelling, "Where's the arm?"

The people next to him chime in, they're getting angry: "Who's she? What's she doing here? Just wait, she'll see! Stupid bitch!"

Stupid, they're right! But raising my arm now won't help, and anyway . . . no. Someone next to me, a gaunt man with a long face, gives me a shove; I fall back against a human wall. The wall seems to give, a narrow passage opens up, just wide enough for me to push my way through toward the back of the crowd. I can still hear cursing from the front as I'm slowly being pushed and shoved to the back, I don't know how. The crowd is like a living rubber wall, it opens and closes and opens again. I'm being pushed out farther and farther. The mass thins out, now there are only small groups of passersby standing around. Don't run! Walk calmly. Keep going, keep going. Ah, there's the Brandenburg Gate. There's almost no one here, just a few pedestrians. One of them walks by with his collar turned up and doesn't even notice me. Another, his scarf pulled around his neck, is hurrying toward the Reichstag. I catch my breath. The din is a long way off now, and no one knows how I got out of there. I hardly know myself . . . the man with the long face who gave me the first shove . . . ?

And we thought we were prepared. We have a lot to learn, even that there may be a time when we have to raise an arm to save ourselves. There will be great sacrifices. But we can't be afraid now; fear is crippling, and we must make our voices heard.

After all, this can't last for long.

# February 1933

# Who Knows Where This Is

# Going to Lead . . . ?

We distributed all the flyers. A different way now. We left them in entrance halls and pushed them under doors: DEATH TO FASCISM—THE STRUGGLE GOES ON!

Today we met at Hedwig's: there were eight of us. Her apartment is relatively safe; no one knows her. What can we do now? Leftist dailies no longer exist, meetings and rallies are banned. We have to continue publishing our literature and we will distribute it illegally. No one knows what's going to happen from here on in, but one thing is clear: terror is growing. There are rumors about demonstrations in various cities; there are also supposed to have been protest strikes, spontaneous. But here in Berlin?

Overnight, at two factories in Wedding, red banners were hung from chimneys. What courage! No one was caught. There's been talk about acts of sabotage—but no mass action. No general strikes.

Now, most important of all, we cannot lose contact with each other. We'll meet regularly, but only in small groups, no more than five people.

Well-known anti-Fascists will have to leave Kreuzberg for the time being. "They're keeping an eye on you, too," I was warned. "See if you can find a different place to stay for a while. You're too well known around here." Brownshirt attacks on working-class bars and apartments are getting more frequent and more brutal.

Should I really . . . ?

I didn't know Frau Schulz and her sister, but Bruno had mentioned his aunts from time to time. "Maybe they can help," he said. "I'll talk to them this evening.

Frau Schulz, a widow, and her unmarried sister, Fräulein Gust, were both members of a workers' chorus. Apart from that they weren't politically active, nor were they known to have leftist sympathies. Bruno explained the situation to them and they understood. They thought about it and said I should drop by and we could discuss the matter.

What they showed me was a dream come true. Together, the sisters ran a candy shop on Gubener Strasse. The store's customers were for the most part children who bought a few *pfennig's*-worth of candy on the way to school. The sisters didn't live in the building but had a separate apartment nearby. Nonetheless, there were living quarters in the back of the shop. A spacious room, a small kitchen, a kind of bathroom, and all this combined with a second, separate entrance from the stairwell. It was the only apartment on the ground floor. The rent wouldn't be a problem, they explained; they were "letting the apartment" and not giving in to those thugs—well, you understand. But I would have to pay for my own gas. Because no one had ever lived there, the stove was not hooked up to the city service and the only available gas was dispensed, for a few *groschen*, from an automat near the entrance. Inside the apartment there were a big bed and several pieces of old furniture.

Frau Schulz thought it would be best if I came and went through the door leading from the stairwell, infrequently of course, only once a day if possible. Before entering, I could check things out from the other side of the street. In an emergency, but only in an emergency—when there were people standing in the hallway, for example—I could enter the apartment through the shop, or slip out the same way. I couldn't have hoped for a better arrangement.

Of course, I had to have my name and address removed from the police registry in Kreuzberg, if only to avoid causing problems for my landlord there. I was uneasy about this whole process, since the police files contained records of my two arrests for taking part in illegal anti-Fascist demonstrations. But everything went smoothly. Were the police just conveniently overlooking some things rather than helping the Brownshirts?

Now I was illegal.

I took what I needed most from my apartment at Belle-Alliance-Platz to my new lodgings on Gubener Strasse and left everything else with my parents. I picked out a few books that were especially important to me,

*With a cousin (right), Berlin 1930*

but only as many as I could carry without attracting attention. Bruno helped me with the "move," and no one but Bruno and my closest friend, Lucie, was to know my new address. I packed a few brochures, papers, and notes. Then I hid my small typewriter in a shopping bag and covered it with vegetables. These days the police were especially vigilant when it came to typewriters. As if typewriters were solely instruments of high treason. And finally, I took my beloved gramophone and a few records, including my favorite songs from *The Three-Penny Opera* and Marlene Dietrich's "Johnny, When It's Your Birthday."

I asked Frau Schulz and Fräulein Gust if they thought it would be all right for me to slip my sports-club passbook in among the dusty boxes on the top shelf—I couldn't bring myself to throw it away, but it was evidence of my socialist connections. They said: "Yes. Until this is all over, and then we'll take it down and you can go back to your gymnastics." I looked at my union passbook and decided to keep it too; who could know how long this would continue?

When you are living illegally they can't just come and drag you out of your apartment and into a cell, but it is not easy to be illegal. We weren't able to imagine clearly the difficulties we would have to face.

I soon lost my job at the bank where I had been working as a foreign-language secretary. My opinions were well known, and I never made a secret of them. On the contrary. There were pointed remarks that sounded like harmless teasing at first. But the atmosphere grew more hostile, even threatening. I had not yet learned to keep my mouth shut: I got into a heated political argument, and some of my colleagues, who were in a hurry to prove their loyalty to the new Führer, openly threatened to denounce me. That afternoon I left and never came back.

Without papers you cannot get a job. Without papers, without being legally registered at the local police station, there was so little one could do that I was almost in despair. Many of the older people in the union movement had thought carefully about their situations and decided not to live illegally, no matter how much at risk they might be.

Maybe I could find part-time work, something to translate or type. I won't need much, my rent is low, I thought. I can talk to my father too, he'll certainly help me out.

No matter what happened we would have to organize acts of protest. We would have to get out a newspaper before the so-called elections on March 5. A regularly published, illegal newspaper. We could not give in!

In the afternoon, I met with Willi, Kurt, and Max. I had gotten to know them when I joined the Socialist Students' League. The three of them were somewhat younger than I. We had agreed to meet in a small park; I can still see the park in my mind's eye but I no longer remember where it was. At any rate, I know it was not in Kreuzberg, where I could no longer show my face. I was warned again, explicitly: something must have gone wrong, they seem to be looking for you.

We had to find a safe place where we could type and make mimeograph copies. Somehow paper and ink had to be found. Did we have anyone who could draw? Where would we find the money to pay for supplies? We sat on a bench in the small park and talked about how to publish an illegal newspaper without being caught right here. How were we to meet on a park bench without calling attention to ourselves—either by being too loud or having to whisper? How were we to behave normally?

All the while carefully observing everything going on around us, who was passing by, were we being watched. Immediately change the subject if necessary. Laugh from time to time maybe. We planned to meet again in three days, and by then everything would have to be ready. The same time, but in a different park.

My father said he wanted to talk to me, he had business in the city, and we met in the evening at my favorite restaurant, Weiss-Csarda on Kommandantenstrasse. I was looking forward to the chicken goulash, the best in Berlin, genuine Hungarian goulash. And today, since my father was paying, I could afford it.

I told him about my problems: no job, not registered, so I'd only be able to find part-time work. I needed money to live on. Not much, I could get along with very little: with a small monthly stipend from him everything would work out. How much could I expect, I asked my father.

"You are mistaken. We cannot give you any financial help at all," he said. "You have to understand that."

I looked at him, confused. I knew him, and I knew it wasn't easy for

*My parents, January 1933, in Berlin*

him to say no to me. But there was no misunderstanding the tone of his voice: he had meant what he said.

"Why?"

"Because we can't." Over the past few weeks they, my mother and father, had devoted considerable thought to whether or not they wanted to stay in Berlin, given the current situation. Yes, it was true, they had just moved into a new apartment, as a precaution. But things were beginning to look more and more worrisome, much worse than they ever could have imagined. He could no longer breathe freely in this country, and he was looking for a job abroad. His company had assured him that they would be of assistance at one or another of their branch offices. This would be best for him, given current circumstances. And, of course, the offer was being made with the understanding that now, in Germany, it would be better for the company to have no Jews in top positions.

My parents' savings would not support them for long; they would have to give up everything they owned in Berlin and leave the apartment, fully paid for one year in advance, leave it and all its contents behind. The landlord's son-in-law had become a storm trooper and let it be known that it was incredibly stupid of Jews not to make an effort to fit in, they were only creating problems for themselves.

Of course they were worried about me. My mother was very upset; her nerves were causing her serious problems. Even Hans was planning to stay only a couple of months longer, until he had completed his doctorate; then he would look for a job in another country, maybe France. For me it would be most reasonable to go with my parents to Prague or Vienna, where I would certainly be able to find a job.

"Impossible! I can't leave now."

"You can't support yourself here. Nothing good can come of your situation. You're only endangering others."

"Are you trying to infect me with your anxieties? Things are most dangerous when you lose your nerve! Is that what you want?"

"Not so loud."

"Father, I can't leave. We can't give in. I am not a deserter."

Herr Weiss walked us to the door. "Herr Direktor," he said, shaking my father's hand, "we're headed for a damned rotten *Szof,* Herr Direktor."

When we were outside I asked my father: "What did he mean? A damned rotten—what is a *Szof?*"

"*Szof* is a Yiddish word. It means 'the end.'"

# "A Sign from Heaven"

# The Reichstag Fire

There were still a few *groschen* in the gas automat and I was at the stove, having just put on water for tea, when I heard the shop door open. I looked up: a gentle knock on the door and Bruno was standing in the hall. What could be going on? He never showed up like this: he always rang twice at the stairwell door, one short and one long. The shop must already be closed! Of course, Bruno had a key. He closed the door behind him and hurried through the hallway into the kitchen. I looked at him and knew that something was wrong.

"Have you heard?" He spoke in a low voice.

"Heard what? What's happened?"

"The Reichstag is burning. Hurry!"

"Hurry, why? What's burning? Did you say the Reichstag?"

"Yes. Listen. They started a fire at the Reichstag and they're trying to pin it on the Communists. 'A sign from Heaven!' Hitler's screaming. This is the beginning, this is the Terror. Forget the tea. Hurry! Do you have anything in your apartment, or on you? I left a few flyers here; do you still have them? Where? We have to get rid of names and addresses first. Is it possible that you've written down any of your meetings? Look through everything in your desk. While you're doing that, I'll go through your books."

We went into the living room and I started pulling the drawers out of my wobbly old desk. Bruno went to the bookshelves.

"Bruno, do you really believe they might be coming here? No one knows about this apartment!"

"Are you sure you haven't hidden any notes in one of these books?" he asked from in front of the shelves. "This apartment—we can never

13

know. You might have a neighbor who's noticed God knows what and wants to make himself appreciated. Do you have literature and brochures anywhere else?"

"No, I'm sure. You're right, we can never know. It's impossible to foresee everything. Here's a piece of paper with the Gesundbrunnen address where we were supposed to be able to set up the mimeograph. Shall I take it with me? No, I'll memorize it, better to get rid of anything that might be used against us."

There was only a small pile of paper that had to be destroyed, we had been careful about the papers we kept. What would be the safest thing to do? We tore everything up into small pieces and flushed them down the toilet. Still, it took some time. We didn't want to flush too often, they might hear the flushing in another apartment, and wonder.

"Now, let's have some tea," said Bruno. "And then I have to go home and clean out my house."

The next day I met with Kurt, Max, and Willi—the "editorial board" is how we referred to ourselves. We all arrived punctually at the agreed-upon park bench, this time in Friedrichshain. It was a part of the park where mostly little children played while being babysat by older siblings—a good, inconspicuous place.

"In Kreuzberg they went at it all night," said Max. Max was about eighteen years old. We called him "Uncle Max," I don't know why. The Nazis knew him by that name too. They had all grown up together and had been schoolmates.

The storm troopers had broken into nearly empty working-class bars—emptied by fear—and had smashed everything to bits with their pistols and knives and clubs. On the streets they beat up everyone who looked like a part of "the Commune." A number of people had suffered knife wounds. The police were nowhere to be seen. Storm troopers charged through the streets, broke down apartment doors where they suspected antifascists to be living, beat family members, destroyed furniture, and carried off the men. We heard they'd been taken to the basement of the SA barracks on Hedemann-Strasse.

"They didn't show up at your place?"

"No. We live closer to Anhalter Station now, the neighborhood's not considered Red."

Willi had heard how viciously 'Storm 33' had charged through Charlottenburg during the night. It was to be expected that this area would suffer the greatest number of casualties. Over the past few weeks the

number of antifascists being murdered had grown—not only Communists, but also more centrist groups like the Reichsbanners.

We quickly agreed to change our plans. Our most important task was
to publish a flyer. The newspaper would have to wait. Something had
gone wrong with the arrangements for the apartment where we were to
set up the mimeograph. But we could screen a flyer immediately. The
headlines read:

WHO ARE THE TRUE ARSONISTS?
WHO ARE THE MURDERERS?
UNITED FRONT AGAINST FASCIST TERROR!

We had to explain how we could protect ourselves against terrorism. But
the problem was just that, how?

The Charlottenburg Antifascist Action had just distributed a flyer a
few days before in which they had continued to call for the formation of
defense committees in each apartment block to combat terrorism. Self-
defense—could that be our answer? Was that possible, reasonable? Yesterday, perhaps. But no longer, not today. Now it was state terrorism we
were confronting.

But the struggle continued.

Willi composed the text for the flyer. Kurt and I produced the flyers.
Uncle Max took over the task of finding a few more people to help with
the distribution.

What we couldn't know was that at this very hour mass arrests had
already begun: all Communist legislators, liberal and Left-leaning intellectuals, writers and artists, and a long list of union leaders—thousands of
people—were taken into "protective custody." We learned about it the
next day.

The distribution of the flyers was a success.

Walter and I had agreed to meet on a corner near Wittenbergplatz at
ten o'clock the next morning. He had let me know that he had something
to discuss with me. I took my windbreaker off the hanger, but then I
thought it over, hung it back up, and put on a light-gray spring coat. Anyone going toward the exclusive Tauenzien district should look as if she
belonged there. Do not attract attention!

After transferring at Gleisdreieck I noticed Appel standing in the
same car, farther down the aisle. He saw me too and walked slowly toward
me until we were standing very close to one another. We both knew that

we shouldn't acknowledge each other in such accidental encounters; it was always possible that one or the other might be shadowed. But these rules were so contrived that no one could live by them, and everyone broke them, despite the horrible dangers the last ten days had shown us.

There are some moments we never forget. I can still see Appel reaching for the strap I was holding onto. He put his other hand into his pants pocket and stood there, nonchalantly, next to me.

Until he looked at me I hadn't noticed how changed he was. Appel— he had gotten his name because of his rosy cheeks and round, childlike face—looked gray. He leaned his head slightly forward and said:

"Have you heard? Erich."

I shook my head and looked at him questioningly. He looks so pained, I thought; and suddenly a fear I had never known before coursed through my body.

"In Spandau."

"Meier?" I asked. I closed my eyes for a few seconds and tried to look as unconcerned as I possibly could.

He nodded. "This morning." It was the eleventh of March.

Appel's eyes wandered over the faces of the passengers in the car.

"Shot. At the sewage dump."

The train stopped. We were at Wittenbergplatz, and I walked quickly to the door and got out. I had to be on time for my meeting with Walter. It was dangerous not to be punctual.

At the time, I wasn't able to get any more details about the murder of Erich Meier. I only found out later.

Walter knew a little coffeehouse on Kleiststrasse where we could get together without being noticed. We hadn't seen each other since January 30, when he had been sitting with the chess players in the café near the Halle Gate.

At first I had trouble following Walter. All I could see before my eyes was Erich, and I just couldn't accept it. Then Walter started talking about the SA cellar on Hedemann Strasse, and I listened. He named friends and comrades who had been dragged in. Some were set free after days of the most vicious torture; they could hardly be recognized. It was from them we learned exactly what was going on there. I listened. I was clenching my hands under the table and felt my fingernails sinking into my palms, but I kept listening. Wasn't there anything we could do?

"That's why I'm here," said Walter, "there's nothing being reported abroad about the barbarism that has come over Germany. Nothing about

Hedemann Strasse, nothing about the hundreds of SA hellholes all over the country. If we can just break through the silence—we can't hope for much, but it would be a powerful strike against the Nazi government if the truth about the torture and the murders were to come out. It just might have an effect."

"But there are foreign correspondents here!" I said. "Where are their eyes?"

"They're blind; they're deaf and dumb. Maybe they don't want to see. Maybe they've been intimidated. Or no one abroad wants to hear anything about this: they don't want to disrupt diplomatic relations. But we shouldn't make it any easier for them."

An old school friend of Walter's was working in a South American consulate. He was able to send material out of the country in diplomatic pouches, and he was prepared to include our literature. From there it would be sent abroad and distributed to press agencies in various countries.

"I want to help," I said.

"We have to meet with the people who've been let out, or with others close to them," said Walter, "being extremely careful, of course. Whenever possible we should get written reports directly from them. Or they must talk to us, and we'll listen very closely but take as few notes as possible. Photographs are important: the open wounds, the bloody clothing."

"Yes, I understand," I interrupted, and I thought, I can do it, I can listen to these people without trembling. But at this moment, under the table, my hands were cold and sweaty.

And why they would let some people go and keep others imprisoned?

"The ones they're letting go, after they've tortured them," Walter said, "are the less-well-known antifascists. The SA are packing more and more people into their cellars, they have to make room. And there can be no doubt that they are hoping the entire population will be intimidated when they see these beaten prisoners."

Walter had agreed to meet a young man at five o'clock in the afternoon. Following his imprisonment in the Hedemann Strasse, this young man had been turned over to the police, who then set him free. Walter suggested that this time we should both meet with him, and I agreed. However, for me this meant wandering around the city for hours in order to avoid going in and out of my apartment too often. Recently I had had to spend a number of days this way; this was the life of an illegal. A day

like this was always difficult: walking, wandering from one part of a
department store to another, always staying alert to what was happening
around you, trying to behave like an ordinary customer. Get a sandwich
in a shop and drink a cup of coffee, then sit as long as possible without
being noticed. Walk again, rest on a park bench and read a newspaper,
then ride around on the U-Bahn for a while, not falling asleep! Always
paying attention. A day that seems like it will never end!

   Then we met in a bar near Treptow Park. Walter knew the young
man by sight: he called him Franz. I didn't learn his real name, I still don't
know it. I was surprised at how much older he seemed than I had imagined him. Maybe it was because of his labored walk. We sat down at a
table, off in a corner where we could talk. I noticed how his gray eyes
twitched and blinked continually. He talked. And for the first time I heard
what it was really like, from someone who had been there, and I had to
commit every detail to memory.

# A Visitor
# from Czechoslovakia.

# The Day of the Jewish
# Boycott

Lucie came by that morning. We had agreed that my parents would
contact me through her whenever they needed to speak with me.

"Your cousin Fritz, from Czechoslovakia, just showed up at your parents'. He'd like to see you too," she reported.

That was a surprise! Someone from another country, my redheaded
cousin from Leitmeritz. He was younger than I. Why was he putting in
an appearance now? Well, naturally I wanted to see him, we would certainly have a lot to talk about. I wanted to know what people abroad had
been hearing about events in Germany. What was being reported in the
papers? Fritz and I had always understood each other very well, we liked
to talk to each other about all kinds of things.

"Do you know how long he's going to stay?" I asked.

"Just a few days."

Then I should go right away. While I was getting ready Lucie played
a few records. I knew which records she'd choose even before she put
them on: as always, Lotte Lenya would come first, singing "Seeräuber
Jenny." One more cup of coffee and we were on our way, ambling along
to the U-Bahn just as we used to do in Kreuzberg. We shouldn't really
have been seen together as often as we were, not even in this neighborhood;

it was not without danger. But in these past few weeks being together had become more important than ever; personal contacts helped to sustain us in our illegal existence.

I took the train to Charlottenburg. Right now, going to my parents' apartment on the Lietzensee probably wasn't very smart either. But it was impossible to avoid every danger. You just couldn't continually suppress everything that was a natural part of your life. We were surrounded by the everyday world, on the train, in the parks, everywhere; but we were bound by unnatural rules. And even if you succeeded in obeying all of them, you still hung by a slender thread called chance.

Anyway, maybe things weren't as dangerous as I was imagining them

*My mother and I, Berlin 1930*

to be. No one knew about the apartment, no one would look for me there. And I had to see Fritz to find out what had brought him here. Who knows, I might even be able to set up foreign contacts through him. Of course I had to go. Talking on the telephone would have been impossible.

When I walked into the apartment Fritz was talking with my parents. He had come by bicycle, at his father's request, as fast as he could. His father, our Uncle Robert, had sent him to persuade our family to come to their house in Leitmeritz as quickly as possible; the house was large enough for all of us. Fritz was to make clear how untenable the situation had become for us in Germany; Uncle Robert assumed we did not have as clear a perspective as he had from outside the country. My parents and I looked at each other. Then they told me they had decided to accept Uncle Robert's offer. They would leave in a few days and hoped that I would reconsider and either leave with them or follow soon after.

"What? You want to go now? And just leave everything here?" I shouted. "The apartment? The books? The record collection you love so much?"

"Have you heard about the day to 'Boycott the Jews'? It's being planned for April first," my mother said. "I can't stay in this country. I just cannot."

"Everything else has become unimportant," said my father, "even the records." My brother, Hans, would stay a while longer, the lease had been paid up in advance.

I asked Fritz if he had had any trouble crossing the border.

No, he had gotten right through on his bicycle. But the following day, on his way into the youth hostel in Luckenwald, he had failed to notice that a company of Brownshirts was also spending the night there. In order not to call attention to himself he had taken part in a study group where the theme was "Weapon 98." Then he followed a torchlight parade in honor of Hitler's meeting with Hindenburg in the crypt of the Potsdam Garnisonskirche. Seeing the quivering bellies of goose-stepping troops snap in step, Fritz had started to laugh. He had forgotten that he was in the Third Reich. But he was reminded by a good shove in the ribs administered by someone standing right next to him.

When he arrived in Berlin he found our Steglitz apartment empty. What had happened? How was he going to find us? He remembered one of our neighbors whom he had met on a earlier visit, and Fritz turned to him. This Dr. Glaubauf seemed very wary. He said he didn't know our new address but would try to get it, and told Fritz to come back the next day.

Then Fritz needed a place to stay for the night. There was no hostel close by, but he was told about a dormitory for unemployed youths. He could spend the night there. After the doors were closed and the boys had lain down on their cots, someone began to sing. Quietly at first, then the others joined in, more and more voices, getting stronger and stronger. Fritz was astounded! Here, at the center of the Third Reich, a leftist anthem:

> *Brothers, to the sun, to freedom!*
> *Brothers, into the light!*

They sang for a long time; they sang freedom songs, and no one tried to stop them.

Some forty years later when Fritz and I recalled these events, he said, "Those songs lingered on in the middle of naked terror, but then they soon died out." I told him back then, "We've been searching for contacts with groups like that, and you, you come from Leitmeritz on your bicycle, and they fall right into your lap."

The next day Fritz went back to Steglitz, and this time Dr. Glaubauf gave him my parents' new address on Suarez-Strasse, in Charlottenburg. He said he'd met my father by chance the previous evening. Actually, he had asked my parents, as a precaution, whether he should give their address to their nephew. That's how Fritz found them and was able to carry out his assignment to plead with them to flee Germany.

I asked what had shaken his father so suddenly and moved him to make his urgent invitation. How much did people there really know about conditions here? About the Terror? I found out that, until now, Uncle Robert, the chief federal judge of the district, had believed that the rumors he was hearing from the other side of the border were no more than gross exaggerations, such atrocities were simply not possible. But then he had read an article in a respected Prague newspaper, a report detailing the lawlessness, the torture, and the anti-Semitism. The article had distressed him deeply. I listened—did this mean that people in other countries really were hearing us? In that case our work would not be in vain.

We talked for a long time and would gladly have talked more, but it was already late afternoon and I had things to do. We had produced flyers, and I had to pick them up and deliver packets to three different friends who had taken the responsibility for distribution. But I hadn't

*Fritz Schalek on the way from Leitmeritz to Berlin*

brought my bicycle. I asked Fritz if I could use his. He said, yes of course, and then added: "Maybe I can help?"

I thought for a moment. It would be easier if there were two of us. Fritz could wait with the bicycle and the packets while I went up and down stairs delivering the flyers to the various addresses, and I wouldn't have to lug the whole lot with me. Above all, it was safer. But could I allow him to help?

"Fritz," I said, "I'm delivering illegal literature. You know what that can mean? Maybe you should stay out of this."

"I understand," he said. "But I want to help. I want to help, very much."

In the meantime it had gotten dark. We rode off, with me sitting on the crossbar. There were no great distances to cover; we picked up a shopping bag containing three smaller packages and cycled to our drop-off points. Each time, as I was climbing the steps to the apartments and Fritz was waiting outside with the flyers, I kept hoping: if we can just get this done without being caught; I should never have gotten him into this.

I could not relax until we were back in the apartment two hours later. One more successful operation!

We agreed to use his home address in Czechoslovakia as a foreign contact point. Uncle Robert, the judge, wouldn't have to know anything about it.

My parents must have been preparing themselves for this all along. They left a few days later.

As I was crossing Alexanderplatz on the first of April, I noticed a crowd of people gathering near the U-Bahn station at the other end of the square. The loudspeakers blared across the open space, "Don't buy from Jews!" They must have been barking out other slogans, too, but I couldn't understand them.

I went closer. Brown uniforms formed two long columns along the sidewalk in front of the entrance to a small shoe store. A Star of David had been smeared across the display window. No one was going in, still the Brownshirts yelled and screamed, waving placards with the slogan "*Juda Verrecke!* Jews Rot!" People stood around and gawked.

Through the glass door of the shop, somewhat blurred, I saw a slender young man. He seemed frightened, or was that just my imagination?

I pushed my way through the crowd up to the Brownshirts and began to walk slowly down the middle of the two rows they had formed. They stared at me and seemed for a moment to be confused. Then one of them yelled again, "Don't buy from Jews!" and the others chimed in. I was almost halfway along through the columns when, from my right, someone whispered in my ear: "Are you crazy? Get out of here!" I saw the new boots, the brown uniform, and a face that looked familiar—but where had I seen it? It must have been at some meeting. A turncoat, one of those who said, "Now we'll just have to go along." I must keep his face in my mind. I walked on, went up the steps to the shop entrance, and went in. Behind me, thunderous screams.

The owner of the shop—or was he an employee?—looked at me, terrified. He tried to pull himself together, and said, "How can I help you?"

"Excuse me," I said, "I don't need any shoes, I don't even have any money. I only came in here so you would know that you're not alone. But give me a pair of shoes to try on, size 36, and then I'll go." I sat down.

The man looked ill. He brought out several boxes, I saw how his hands were trembling, and my anger rose.

"You shouldn't have done this," the young man said in a low voice.

When I was outside again I walked back through the two columns. I looked straight ahead, closed my ears to the screams, and continued on across the Alex in the direction of the police presidium. As I walked I thought to myself, How could you have done that? You're illegal.

# EASTER

It was already a month since we had started working on our newspaper. We had to keep putting it off; and after everything that had happened in this one month, we had to start over from the beginning again.

First: where could we work? Everything was becoming so much more difficult. We couldn't work in a park. Or in a bar. In an apartment? Whoever was living legally was living at an unsafe address.

"You can meet somewhere in the area," Bruno suggested. "In one of the 'better' neighborhoods, on a weekday, but only two at a time, like lovers."

And where could I find a typewriter? In my quarters on Gubener Strasse someone might notice the excessive typing. In an apartment building there are always curious people who notice anything unusual.

Bruno had an answer for everything: he was in contact with someone in Gesundbrunnen who had a typewriter, and I could type the mimeo masters there. Possibly even that same day or the next, so I wouldn't have to carry everything around with me for very long.

On Wednesday morning, at ten o'clock, I met Kurt in the U-Bahn station at Onkel-Toms-Hütte, and we left together going toward Krumme Lanke. This was my turf, I knew every inch of it. In the past we had gone bicycling here, and swimming. It was still cool, but the sun was shining. The deeper we went into the woods, the lonelier it got. We saw hardly anyone.

We found an out-of-the-way spot under a big tree and sat down; the trunk provided us with some cover. The ground was still moist from the dew, and I spread out my coat before sitting down. I lay down on my stomach and held my tablet under my chest so I could hide it very quickly if that became necessary. We spoke quietly, and while I wrote, Kurt's eyes kept sweeping the landscape. It seemed to be a relatively safe place and our work progressed well and quickly—there was so much that had to be said.

"Someone's coming!" said Kurt in mid-course. I quickly pushed the tablet under my stomach and then looked up. Now I could hear footsteps too.

An older man in a coat and hat, carrying a cane, appeared on the path and strolled slowly past.

". . . and they gave me today off, but I have to go back to the office tomorrow," I said.

"But on the weekend we'll take a little trip somewhere," Kurt answered. He squeezed up closer to me and put his arms around my shoulders.

No, this was no stool pigeon, this walker with his rather wobbly gait, and he certainly was no Brownshirt. He briefly looked our way and then went on. We continued to discuss the coming weekend, and I giggled a little until the old guy had disappeared. No reason to get nervous, just keep calm, why shouldn't a gentleman of somewhat advanced years be strolling by here? Still . . . .

"Let's take a break," I said to Kurt, who was ready to keep working. "He might come back."

But he didn't come back. No one else passed by either, and we continued to work for a long time. We stood up from time to time only to stretch our limbs.

Finally, we went back to the Krumme Lanke train station together, our arms around one another as a precaution, and took separate trains back home. I carried the steno notes under my blouse.

The next morning, Thursday, at five minutes after ten, I was at the Friedrichstrasse Station, as agreed. I was again carrying the notepad under my blouse. Bruno had organized everything. Maria was to meet me here and take me to an apartment where I would be able to type.

I walked slowly up and down the platform looking around for Maria. I had met her through Bruno. She was plump, had dark-blond hair, and was a few years older than I. Clearly she hadn't yet arrived. All of a sudden I spotted Walter. Walter? He was sitting alone on a bench. What was *he* doing here? He must have already seen me because he nodded my way, imperceptibly. Actually we shouldn't acknowledge one another. But it was Walter after all! I stood for a moment, looked around, and then walked slowly over to the bench and sat down next to him without saying a word.

"Are you taking this train north too?" he asked.

"Yes."

"You're waiting for someone?"

"Yes. And you?"

"Me too. So we'll go together."

I looked at the station clock. It was now nine minutes after ten. I looked around once more, but Maria still hadn't arrived. Well, okay, four minutes, we couldn't always be that precise.

"You're waiting for Maria?" I nodded. "Certainly be here soon," said Walter.

We sat next to one another and kept silent. A train pulled in, and I looked toward the doors and the people getting off. Someone plump and dark-blond? Here . . . no, that definitely wasn't her. I shouldn't be paying so much attention to hair color, because Maria had a pageboy and might be wearing a hat. We had all begun to wear hats, because they gave us such a solid bourgeois look. But Maria was not among the disembarking passengers.

I looked up at the big clock again. It was fifteen minutes past ten. I was beginning to feel uneasy. I looked at Walter sitting next to me, completely relaxed.

There was no one within hearing distance. "We shouldn't wait more than ten minutes," I said.

"Right . . . theoretically. But things don't always work out that way. If you follow all the rules so closely you won't get anywhere."

We waited.

"Eighteen minutes past ten," I said.

"Just a bit longer," said Walter. "She has to show up soon. I have to get there today, no matter what, I can't put it off any longer."

"Ten-twenty. That's fifteen minutes late."

"Listen," said Walter. "I know the apartment, I was there once. I don't know the address, but I can remember the street and the building exactly, and I know I can find it. Something must have happened to Maria, but we can go there even without her. What do you think?"

"No. Never! You know that's the kind of thing that'll get one of us yanked. We've waited twenty minutes here, something's wrong, that's clear. We have to get out of here."

"You're probably right," said Walter. "Yes, probably. It's just that someone's waiting for me there. . . . But you're right, we can't take a chance like that." He hesitated a moment, got up, and walked toward the exit on the right. I waited a while and then got up and headed for the escalator on the left.

Should I go back home now? Maybe it would be better to wait a little longer, after all. Something had gone wrong. And I was standing here with the entire newspaper text under my knit blouse. I had worn it because it was so large that nothing under it would show.

I walked around for a while in the direction of the Lustgarten. I could go to the museum. But, now especially, the museum didn't interest me in the least. I didn't feel well, I had a headache. I continued walking and came to the Alex, sat down at an Aschinger coffee stand and drank a cup of coffee. My headache wouldn't go away. What could have happened to Maria? Maybe I was exaggerating; maybe it was just something unexpected, something entirely harmless that had kept her from showing up, that was always possible. Uh, I should just go back home and lie down.

Back on Gubener Strasse, I could see through the display window that there were people in the candy shop: a woman with two children. So I went around to the outside entrance. In the hallway I stopped and looked around for a moment. Careful! I told myself. It was quiet in the stairwell, and I walked cautiously down the hallway to my apartment door, put my key into the lock, turned it slowly, and opened the door a crack. Hadn't I heard something? I was terrified. In the semidarkness I thought I saw someone standing at the door. I cringed. Is this happening . . . happening, now?

"It's me," said Bruno's voice, before I could close the door from the outside. As he shut the door behind me I could see his hand trembling on the knob.

"You're back!" he said hoarsely.

"Yes, what's happening, why are you here?" My voice didn't seem to want to produce the words. "I was waiting for Maria."

"She didn't come?" he asked nervously. "So, she's holding up!"

"You know something? What's happened?"

"Maria is in the apartment with the typewriter." He took me by the arm and led me into the room, and I could sense him trying to keep calm. "She's being held there by the Gestapo and they're waiting for one of us, any one of us, to show up. They haven't been able to get her to talk, otherwise they'd have grabbed you at the Friedrichstrasse Station. No one knows who else might have fallen into this trap. Too many people knew about the apartment."

"Where did you find all this out?"

"Someone went there, could tell something was rotten, and was able to get away."

"And what now?" I said. "Is there anyone else we can warn? Can we help Maria? And what about the newspaper, the text, where can I type it? Is there anyone they've got who knows my address?" Thoughts whirled around in my head. "This headache. It's as if someone were hitting me over the head with a hammer. I have to lie down. Can't you stay a while longer, Bruno?"

I took an aspirin, lay down on the bed, and must have fallen asleep immediately.

When I woke up my head was clearer. Bruno was still there. There was only one possibility: I had to type out the masters for the newspaper here in my apartment. We put a thick blanket under the typewriter to deaden the sound. And we played loud music on the gramophone to cover up the sound of the clicking keys.

"Here," said Bruno, and he pulled a record out of the stack, "The Triumphal March from *Aïda*! That'll make some noise."

I had an adequate supply of mimeo masters hidden behind the books. Bruno put on *Aïda*, I started to type, and when the march was over, Bruno cranked up the machine and played *Aïda* over again, from the beginning. It was ringing in my ears, and I typed as fast as I could, thinking all along, if I ever manage to finish this, and this is all past, I will never want to hear *Aïda* again. I don't want to hear anybody's Triumphal March, ever again, for the rest of my life.

It was four pages long. First we destroyed my steno notes, and then I got on my bicycle and took the masters, in a shopping bag, to Kurt, who would run off the copies. Exactly as planned: Thursday evening.

Kurt said he didn't need any help with production. But we had to find new people to help with the distribution. We had lost too many. Uncle Max, for example, had to stay out of sight.

"What happened? Is he safe?"

"The Brownshirts hunted all through Kreuzberg for him. Now he's with friends in a tent encampment."

Most of these camps were near lakes in the region and had come into being over the past few years. Many jobless young people spent their summers in the tents and did what they could to help each other get along; sometimes they got eggs and milk, or even day work, from nearby farmers. Neither the SA nor the Gestapo had been paying any attention to the tent camps, so they still provided a safe haven for many fugitives.

Now we needed new people to help with the distribution of our literature. Kurt reported that Willi had found a few young friends who wanted to take part.

Why was it always young people? The "old ones," the ones with so much experience—weren't they going to join us?

Kurt and his father had had a falling out. Kurt's father was an old union man who had fought many battles. "What you're doing is not just nonsense," he had said to Kurt, "it's unconscionable. Illegal work is useless now, it only multiplies the number of victims, and what's going to become of their families? You have no right to do this!"

I couldn't get it out of my mind—what Kurt's father had said. He was wrong! Were we supposed to keep quiet in the face of this criminality? And would no one tell the truth? Would there be no resistance?

We should give in?

We didn't give in.

We had always spent Easter vacation traveling with friends. Some felt we should do the same this year. Get together again. Talk about what had been happening, what is going to happen, and what we can do. And, as Bruno's friend Karl had suggested, maybe we would hear a lecture on historical materialism. Isn't that too risky, getting together openly in large groups, for political discussions? others asked. Most, however, were only concerned that it be well organized. At Easter there were many groups of young people traveling to the countryside and sleeping in tents or youth hostels. We wouldn't be at all conspicuous, so long as we made our plans carefully. This time we could even go a bit farther away, maybe to one of the lakes in Mecklenburg, where so many young people spent their holidays.

There were about twenty of us who wanted to go: young antifascists who belonged to different groups, some individuals, too—comrades who had known each other for a long time and were continuing the struggle.

We took the train in groups of two or three; all we had been told was where we were to get off. At this point we would be met by a friend on the platform who would give us directions to our campsite. Lucie, Bruno, and I traveled together. For three whole days we would be out in the fresh air, able to relax! Three days on the water, with friends, in the sun. Far away from the city and its threats. Escaping from the enforced isolation that was so hard on us. We would talk about our experiences, about the dangers, the successes and failures, we would talk about our mistakes and learn from one another.

A number of tents had already been put up around the lake, young people were everywhere. Everything was as it had been in the past: there was a group of scouts, and beyond them the "wilde Clique," an anarchistic bunch of nature lovers in their usual attire. There were no brown uniforms here. We put up our big round tent near the water. I ran down to the shore with a few others and jumped into the lake. The water was cool, it felt good; we swam a long way out.

Then we lay in the sun and I looked up toward our tent to see who else had come. I had completely lost contact with many of them over the past few months. I saw Kurt and Else arrive, and I thought of the night of the torchlight parade, when we had last sat together eating liver pasties in the little café near the Halle Gate. Willi was here, and Paul, and Karl. But many were missing. I knew that a couple of our chess players had been arrested early on.

We could hear the hum of voices coming from our tent farther up the hill. It got louder. I listened.

". . . so it's not a defeat we've suffered? Man, that's a lot of bullshit. Who are you trying to put on anyway?"

"The union didn't fight because the time wasn't right for a fight." I recognized Willi's voice. "It was a tactical retreat and not a loss. We are still here, after all. But we're no thrill-seekers; an uprising would have led to useless bloodshed."

"And what about the blood that's being shed today—now, when we can no longer defend ourselves?" That was Karl's raised voice.

"We are defending ourselves politically!" shouted Willi.

That was much too loud! I ran up the hill with two others.

"Do you want to get us all arrested right here?"

The discussion had become so heated that the comrades had forgotten all caution. They were shocked when we jumped in.

Something like this just couldn't be allowed to happen. Nothing was as it had been before, no matter where we were. From then on we posted guards during political discussions. From time to time we sang old folksongs. Do not attract attention, do not talk too loudly, and do not under any circumstances whisper secretively!

"This holds for the lecture on historical materialism, too, early tomorrow," said Karl.

"I don't know if the lecture is such a good idea," said Lucie. "As if we weren't already in enough danger without historical materialism. More theory now, of all times?"

But most of us agreed that now it was especially important not to neglect our theoretical foundations, after all, our convictions were our strength. . . . Where else would we find courage in the face of such terror . . . ?

"Now, to get on with our work, to our immediate problems. What should we do about comrades who've just been released from camps or prison; shouldn't they be put on ice, at least for a while? There are turncoats and there are traitors, are they one and the same? And how should we treat people who simply are no longer strong enough to continue?"

"Even caution can be exaggerated to the point where one can hardly distinguish it from cowardice. On the other hand, there is a lot of stupidity and it has already cost too many lives. The decision—what to do and what not to do—is an individual one, and it is difficult. Last week I was about to go to a meeting; but when I heard it was to be at the house of a Jewish doctor who had already fled, a doctor who was being sought by the SA, supposedly because he had been performing abortions, I refused to go and demanded that the meeting be ditched. You can imagine the critical stares that came my way!"

But how is it possible to obey the rules of illegal life when everything normal strains against them? Erich Meier, who had organized the Spandau Self-Defense Group—his composure was an example to all of us. But would the SA have been able to search him out in the Good Hope gardens and haul him off to the sewage fields if he hadn't left his Berlin hideout and returned to Spandau? He couldn't stand the isolation any more, he couldn't take being a spectator, simply handing over power to the fascists without a fight. And besides, he had to see his girl again. . . . We're all human beings. Erich had always said: "They won't break me that easily. I know how to take care of myself, I've already proved it to them."

When Marta Fittko saw Erich entering her produce shop, she hissed at him,"Kid, what are you doing here, they're going to kill you!" But Erich shook his head, smiled at her, and went on his way.

You hadn't expected a traitor. That was back in March. More than a thousand Spandauers came to your burial.

We talked about this and many other things on our Easter holiday.

# CHARLOTTENBURG—WEDDING —NEUKÖLLN

The weather was getting warmer and I had to go to my parents' apartment on the Lietzensee to pick up some lighter clothes. Most of what I had with me on Gubener Strasse were winter clothes, because I had thought back then: This cannot last forever. But now it was the end of April. You had to dress well in order to avoid attracting attention. Up to this time nothing had happened at my parents' apartment; it would not be particularly dangerous to go there.

We sat at the table in the dining room: my brother, Hans, his girlfriend, Eva, and I. Eva had brought something to eat. We had also managed to dig up a bottle of Rhine wine and had drunk almost all of it. Now I was tired.

"Today is April 28," I said. It had just occurred to me.

"So?" asked Hans.

"Silver wedding anniversary."

Except for birthdays we celebrated very few events in our family, but we had planned to prepare a little surprise for our parents on this occasion. Now the day had come and we were not spending it together.

"Let's send them a telegram—that's something we can still do," said Hans. "We can phone it in."

"Good—maybe a little joke, something to make them laugh?"

From time to time when our parents had a falling out, our father would try to relieve the tension, sighing deeply, "The countless hours of agony I have suffered since we married. . . ." That's it, we could calculate how many hours there were in twenty-five years. Or how many minutes!

Hans went to get his slide rule. He miscalculated a couple of times and had to start over from the beginning, but finally, with Eva's help, he was able to work out the answer. We composed the telegram: "CONGRAT-ULATIONS ON HAVING SUCCESSFULLY SURVIVED THE FIRST THIRTEEN MIL-LION ONE HUNDRED AND FORTY THOUSAND MINUTES OF AGONY."

I phoned in the text to have it sent to Czechoslovakia, and we laughed and imagined how amused our parents would be. Then we made coffee. As I was getting the cups out of the china cabinet, I remembered the lit-tle drawer that held a dozen gold coffee spoons. Or were they teaspoons? I couldn't remember our ever having used them. Once I had asked my mother about them and all she had said was, "Nonsense, who needs gold spoons? Besides, they're not even very pretty." Maybe someone had given them to my parents as a wedding gift? But now I took three of them out and set them on the table with the coffee, and we laughed again: now, of all times, gold spoons!

The telephone operator was probably still shaking her head over that crazy telegram. What will they think of next!

Or—it really was a very unusual message. Might the operator some-how come to the conclusion that this was a secret code . . . ?

At any other time we would probably have thought this terribly silly, but now. . . . It had not occurred to us that even a harmless joke like this one could be dangerous. No sooner do you let your guard down than you make a big mistake. We sat there for a while, thinking. If we were inter-rogated, all we would have to do is tell the truth. Explain that the telegram was a joke. They could do their own calculations and see. But once you attract their attention. . . .

"Maybe you should leave," Hans said to me.

I got up. The telephone rang and I reached for the receiver without thinking.

"Hello?"

"This is the operator." Was that really possible? I sensed Hans's and Eva's eyes on me. Just keep calm.

"Yes?"

"Did you just phone in a telegram for Czechoslovakia?"

"Yes."

"Excuse me, but the telegram has not yet been sent."

"Why not?"

"I hope you won't be upset with us. We had so much fun with it here, all of us, and then we made our own calculation, and sure enough, we found a mistake. You forgot to include leap year! And so we thought we should correct it; it should be accurate, shouldn't it?" The operator laughed good-naturedly. I laughed too; of course it would be a pity if the whole thing were inaccurate, and I thanked her and asked her to include the leap-year minutes.

I hung up and explained, and we laughed again—but no longer so freely, this time more like someone weak in the knees.

As I was walking home, heading toward Kantstrasse, I heard steps behind me. A man's footsteps following steadily in my path, keeping a fixed distance—no faster, no slower than my pace. Had the apartment been under surveillance after all? And was I being shadowed? I slowed down, the footsteps behind me slowed down. In front of a small bookshop I hesitated as if to look at the books on display. And the steps came more slowly and someone stopped behind me, I could see a tall man with a hat reflected in the store window. I looked at the books and thought for a while. Then I turned around suddenly, all but bumping into the man, looked him straight in the eye, and quickly crossed the street. I turned into a side street and slowly continued on my way. No, now no one was following me, no steps behind me. This had been nothing more than a little game. You wouldn't be able to get rid of the Gestapo or the Nazis so easily. But maybe I was beginning to imagine things. It wouldn't have been the first time a man had followed a woman in Berlin.

I had asked my brother how he was doing financially, and if he could help me out. But he couldn't, he had almost nothing himself. He was planning to go abroad soon and would try to make his way somehow. Many of his university friends were already in Paris. He was only waiting to take the oral exam for his doctorate. In the meantime he would have to accept an offer from a friend's parents to move in with them in their house on the Wannsee. A friend and fellow student by the name of Fahrenhorst had also offered to help him out financially.

There was to be nothing for me from that quarter. Up until this time I had been doing some translation work, but the circle of people with whom I had contact was growing smaller and smaller. My cousin's wife Anni invited me to eat with them whenever I could. My cousin was a diplomat, and I was as safe with them as I possibly could be in those days. And a few of my friends who had jobs sometimes gave me a little money. All in all, it was a very shaky existence—and I had no idea how it would continue.

I had agreed to meet Alfred on Thursday, at two o'clock in the afternoon.

We had met at a sports club. He was from Wedding, and I knew that he was continuing to work there illegally. The resistance in Wedding had been seriously weakened because of a large number of recent arrests and, more and more, communications were breaking down. Because I knew people there, Alfred had asked me to help set up new contacts.

On Wednesday, when I saw Kurt, he gave me the same news about Kreuzberg: a lot of people had been caught and communications among the rest had broken down. New channels would have to be opened.

"There's a meeting at Hedwig's tomorrow afternoon at two. I'll be seeing a couple of the people who are still active," Kurt said. "You have to be there, you know our friends in Kreuzberg."

I said, "I can't go tomorrow, I have another meeting."

We thought it over. Yes, of course, to me Kreuzberg was more important, because it's where I could be of most help. But I couldn't just leave Alfred in the lurch, put him at risk, lose contact with him. It was impossible to phone or write a card. . . . Then I thought of Willi. He knew Alfred and I could reach him through his family. I would ask him to go in my place.

Willi agreed. He would go, even if only to make sure we didn't lose contact with Alfred. We were to meet at a busy intersection somewhere on Brunnenstrasse. It was safer that way, you could simply disappear into the crowd if there was anything amiss.

The meeting at Hedwig's went well; no one was discouraged despite the arrests. But from now on we would have to be more vigilant and work more cleverly. Of course we would continue—restore communications, maintain them, distribute our antifascist literature.

On that same evening I received a warning. Stay away from everyone. Stay out of sight. Willi was arrested in Wedding. Wait and see if he can hold out.

Alfred must have been arrested sometime between Tuesday, when we had last met, and Thursday. Maybe they had tortured him and he had weakened. Or maybe he had written down the location and they had found the note in his apartment. And that's why Willi had been arrested. Instead of me. Maybe he had given Alfred a sign when he saw him approaching. After all, Alfred hadn't known that Willi was coming in my place. I imagined what had happened: Alfred had been forced to go to meet me.

The Gestapo officers followed him, observing everything very carefully; at the least suspicion they would strike. Willi saw Alfred coming but didn't notice that Alfred was being shadowed. The only thing the Gestapo could have forced out of Alfred was a description of *me*. Still, they must have noticed that Willi and Alfred knew each other—one look, a hand movement might have been enough—and at that moment they struck, before Willi could run.

Terrible questions went through my mind: What are they going to do to him? They will do to him what they would have liked to do to me, though I cannot imagine that they will be able to break him down. One must always, in every instance, protect oneself. One can never know who has the strength. . . . It is not a matter of physical strength . . . not even necessarily, as we have seen, the strength of one's convictions. . . . Do I know how strong I am? But, stop, this is nonsense, one cannot afford to doubt oneself. . . . For now, I would have to hibernate for at least ten days.

"We can't even make rhubarb compote this year," Lucie complained. "Where could we cook it? And where are we going to find all the sugar?" Lucie lived in Berlin-Center and I couldn't go there. And in my part of the city, on Gubener Strasse, we couldn't afford to do anything that would attract attention. And rhubarb season would soon be over.

A few days later Lucie started talking about rhubarb again: we could make compote at Käthe's. Käthe lived in Neukölln, where no one knew us. Of course, the apartment wasn't totally safe because Käthe's father was a Communist. But Lucie said: "We can't give up everything in life, and rhubarb just happens to be a part of life. And you have to get out of that hiding place once in a while. And anyway, Käthe's managed to come up with some sugar."

"We need a lot!" I said. "Otherwise it will be too sour."

"We've got enough sugar for an entire army," she reassured me.

Good, then off to Neukölln. Lucie brought the rhubarb; donated by a neighbor with a garden. We sat around Käthe's kitchen table, cleaning, cutting, and talking about things we had heard. Who had been nailed. Who had been taken to Oranienburg. Who had escaped abroad. And whom we could not trust.

Käthe's little niece, Anita, came in, and we let her help. She must have been about five years old then; we all referred to her as "our baby." She stirred the compote carefully with a large cooking spoon.

"The flags are there again," she said. "In the windows."

"What flags?"

"I don't know. Everybody has them. But not our flags. The other ones."

"You say everybody's flying flags out of their windows. But it can't be everybody!"

"No, but a lot. Aunt Käthe?"

"What, darling?"

"The other kids look at me funny. They wonder why we don't have a flag in our window."

"Do you want us to hang out a flag like theirs?"

"Me? No. I don't really want to. But . . . Aunt Käthe? Couldn't we . . . we could pretend . . . maybe just for now, and then we could take out our own flag. It's in the basement, way in the back, but I never tell anyone."

"Anita, sometimes we have to hide our flag. But to give our flag up for another one—only bad people do that."

"Those other people are pretending too."

"Is that what the kids are saying?"

"Sometimes. And with the other flag we don't have to worry about grandpa all the time!"

"But grandpa would never do that. I'll explain it to you; but first we have to take care of the rhubarb."

"Aunt Käthe, aren't you afraid too?"

Käthe tasted the compote slowly and thoughtfully. "It's getting to be sweet enough. It's almost done." She looked at Anita. "Sweetie, we are doing what honorable people must do, and there's nothing else we can do, whether we are afraid or not."

Lucie took Anita in her arms and danced around the kitchen with her, singing:

> *Freut euch des Lebens*
> *solange der Rhabarber blüht—*
> *Enjoy this life*
> *as long as the rhubarb blooms*

and then we all sang along:

> *Freu dir, Fritzchen, freu dir Fritzchen*
> *Morgen gibts Selleriesalat—*
> *Be happy Fritz, be happy Fritz*
> *Tomorrow we'll have celeriac—*

When the rhubarb was done we called everyone into the kitchen, grandma and grandpa and the whole family. The rhubarb was delicious, sweet and tart and sour.

# The Night of the Census

No new arrests. Willi's not talking. We hear from a friend of his sister's that he's been taken to a police lockup. At least he's not in the hands of the Gestapo anymore!

Alfred was seen in Wedding. Free.

That's how they work, they let people go and then they shadow them. They watch to see whom these people will contact; they wait and they watch. Then they strike: everything is shattered, communications are lost. That's why everyone who's released has to be "put out in the cold" at first. We can't contact Alfred. When we see him we have to look away. Although it's not at all clear that he actually did inform on the meeting with Willi. No, not with Willi, with me; he would have to have assumed that I would be the one to get yanked. . . . Should we have behaved differently? If only I had gone to the meeting instead of sending Willi! But that's crazy. The Terror is guilty, not us. "Don't rush to be with the angels," Kurt always laughed. "Your turn will come." There is a lot of black humor going around, and we laugh; we can laugh about the Terror in spite of everything! We hold up better when we laugh together.

But what if Alfred said nothing, what if they found out about the meeting some other way? What must it be like to be suspected and shut out by your own comrades! To be entirely alone.

I finally felt confident enough to come out of hiding. Since Willi's arrest—except for the rhubarb celebration—I had very rarely gone out on the street. Once or twice maybe, to buy something I needed, or because I simply couldn't take being shut in anymore. Once, in the morning, when no one was on the street, I went out to a little park near my apartment and sat down on a bench with a book. It was Zweig's *Fouché*, and I lost myself in it, living the events on its pages.

Then it occurred to me—This is absurd! We are living in the year 1933. I am living this year hidden here in Berlin East. How can I sit here

41

on a sunny morning in this park and pretend that everything is the way it used to be—reading a book about a man Zweig called "the most remarkable political figure of all time"? And I didn't know whether Zweig's books had been burned in May. I didn't even know whether or not he was a Jew.

Kurt and Else had prepared a new leaflet and we needed more people to help with the distribution. Now we also wanted to produce small handbills, which would be easier to print and disperse; most importantly, this was less dangerous. And we had to develop new methods to get these flyers to the masses without getting caught. Maybe we should scatter them

*Eva Rosenthal and my brother, Hans Ekstein (front row, second and fourth from the left), on the evening before their wedding (Berlin, 1934).*

from a rooftop and let the winds do our work.

One of the times I went to eat with Andre and Anni, my cousin and his wife, my brother was there too. Anni had gone to Leitmeritz for a few days to visit my parents, and she wanted to tell us both about her trip. She had been assigned the task of pressuring us to leave Germany. And she had the money for my ticket—but only if I promised to leave!

"We'll talk about it later," I said.

Hans was getting ready to leave for France. It turned out that he was in more danger than he had first thought. He had been warned not to show himself too often, especially at the university. There was a group of Strasser followers in the Student SA; they believed that nazism could lead the way to socialism. Hans knew a few of them. They had talked politics from time to time, and Hans had even been invited to take part in some of their meetings. And once he had accepted and given a lecture.

After the Nazis took power these contacts were broken off. Hans, Eva, and a few friends continued to keep a small group of antifascist students going, and they had begun to produce flyers and brochures.

A few days before I saw Hans, a student, a stranger to Hans, had come up to him at the university. He said friends of his had mentioned Hans's name—and he rattled off the names of a few Strasser followers. He spoke briefly and asked Hans to meet him in a coffeehouse; he didn't want to be seen with Hans in public.

"I've been asked to warn you," he said, once they were seated in the café. "The Student SA has got you on their list. They've decided to catch you if you show up again at the university. Today you were lucky. But take this warning seriously unless you want to end up on Hedemann Strasse." He stood up, raised his arm, shouted "Heil Hitler!" and left.

A census had been announced. Suddenly, all residents were ordered to be at the address where they were legally registered on the appointed night. Every home would be checked, everyone would be counted.

The census was aimed at us illegals! And this meant that we, the illegals, would have to spend the night in parks, on benches, in dark streets, backyards, and alleys. Stay alert, eyes open, listen, be ready to run. No sleep, not for a moment! We were wild game in season.

"Lucky I've got my room on Gubener Strasse," I said to Lucie as she was walking home with me. "It's just a candy store, no one is registered there, they won't even bother." She was registered at her father's address and would spend the night there.

We went through the hallway into my apartment. I went to the kitchen to put water on, but I couldn't get any gas. Funny, I knew that I had put enough money into the gas automat. I went out to check. The gas automat was locked! That very same moment there was a knock on my door, and Frau Schulz, the store owner, came in.

"I'm very sorry," she began somewhat breathlessly. "I am really very sorry. But you can't stay here tonight, you have to leave."

"Now? Right now?" I stared at her and saw how red her face was. "Because of the census?"

"You're not registered here. What will happen if they come and smash everything to pieces and take us . . . no, really, you can't stay, you can't do this to us . . . do you understand? . . . You've got to understand me!" She was talking faster and faster and getting muddled. "And anyway, it's not just for our sake, it's for you too; if someone here in the building denounces you, and they find you here, what can we do then, my sister and I, how can we explain who you are . . . ?"

"But no one in the building knows you've got someone living in the apartment. No one has seen me coming in here."

"Yes, that's what you believe. And hasn't it occurred to you that the stairwell has ears? I haven't wanted to say anything, but people have asked me about you. People in the building see the light in the apartment, they hear the door. And they ask me why you don't have your name on the door like everyone else."

I wasn't sure whether she had just made this up or whether it was true. Of course it was possible, and she was right, it had really never occurred to me that anyone would notice.

"Come on," Lucie said to me. "Bring what you need for the night. We'll see where we can find a place for you to stay until morning."

"No. That's not what I mean," said Frau Schulz, and her face turned bright red. "Take everything you can take with you now, and pick up the rest later. Maybe Bruno can help. You just can't stay here any longer. I'm sorry, really. I'm worried about you, too, but there's nothing else I can do. You have to understand!"

"Does Bruno know about this?"

"Not yet. He has enough problems of his own tonight."

"Yes," I said, "of course. Yes, I understand. And thank you very much for everything."

"Damn it!" I said to Lucie, when we got outside. "What do you think, shall we go to my parents' place on the Lietzensee and see if we can work something out there?"

Hans was home. He was legally registered. We thought and thought, and he decided it would be best for me to spend the night there. "In back, in the maid's room, next to the kitchen, they probably won't check there. Anyway, I'll figure something out."

After Lucie had gone I cleaned up every trace of my presence, took my things back to the room, and locked the door from the inside. That won't help much, I thought to myself, but at least it will give me a moment's more time.

There was a bed in the room and I lay down. I was exhausted, but I wouldn't get much sleep. . . .

When I heard the doorbell ring, I jumped and looked blearily at my watch. It was six-thirty in the morning. I could hear sounds in the apartment quite clearly. Hans's bedroom door opened; it always creaked a little. I knew he would be putting on his old gray bathrobe with the red stripes. And that was the sound of his slippers shuffling quietly down the hallway to the apartment door.

I lay on the bed completely dressed and motionless. I felt my body stiffen and grow cold. The front door opened and two voices shouted, "Heil Hitler!" Then my brother's voice, "Heil Hitler!" That had an almost calming effect on me, I don't really know why; maybe because it was simply impossible. The door latch closed, steps circulated through the rooms. Now—no, they weren't coming in this direction. I heard voices, but not loud enough to understand. Such a long conversation! Once I heard them laugh. I understood a few words from time to time: "fellow student"—"If you don't mind"—"Excuse me"—"Thank you very much." Then a collective "Heil Hitler!" and the door to the apartment latched shut again. I heard the unmistakable sound of my brother's footsteps coming down the hallway toward the kitchen. He knocked as he went by and said, "You can come out now."

The frozen space around my body began to thaw.

"They're gone?"

"Yes."

"And they're not coming back?"

"No. But now let's have a cup of coffee, and I'll explain." That's my brother Hans; that's the way he is.

He had immediately seen that they were both students. They were wearing SA uniforms. When they asked for his registration papers he just happened to have his student identification ready too. "Ah, a fellow student!" one of them exclaimed; then they introduced themselves, and they all had quite a pleasant conversation. Hans invited them into the living room and they admired the beautiful view of the lake with the weeping willows on both shores. As an aside, they asked who else lived here and Hans explained that his parents were on vacation on the Baltic coast. That was sufficient, thank you. No, they didn't want to search anywhere. "Not here, of all places!" one of them said, and laughed. Then they left.

We had survived. And what now? My brother would soon move into the room that had been offered him in a villa on the Wannsee. The wife of his friend Fahrenhorst would then drive him in their car across the border into France.

I would have to find other quarters for myself quickly.

"I'll talk to Frau Hoffman," I said. "I know her address. Maybe I can stay with her for a while."

For years Frau Hoffman had helped my mother with housekeeping. She was from Pomerania, a widow, and lived with her two sons somewhere in Schöneberg.

"Lisachen!" she said, her bright blue eyes sparkling and her pink cheeks glowing. She wanted to pull me into the parlor, but I told her I would rather stay with her in the kitchen.

"Frau Hoffman, may I stay with you for the time being?" And I explained my situation.

"Oh my, I can't help you there, Lisa. I just can't. You see, it's Klemens, my older son. They're after him. You'd be jumping from the frying pan into the fire."

"Klemens? I always thought he wasn't interested in politics?"

"Well, he's never belonged to a party. He always thought they all talked a good line but never did anything for any of us, just blamed each other for what was wrong, and now we see what's happened. But Klemens never could keep his mouth shut. They were here once already, but they didn't find him. He almost never comes home himself—so, you see, I can't help you, Lisachen, you should follow your parents. Things are not going to go well here."

Later I met Bruno in Treptow. "You have to get out of here," he said.

Three of our new people had been arrested for distributing leaflets. The very first time! Kurt and I had met with them a few days before, we had discussed everything in detail. All three of them were young, they were full of impatience and wanted, no matter what the risk, to be part of the resistance against the fascist thugs.

Kurt had told Bruno about the arrests. One of the boys had been able to smuggle a note out with his mother: the boys had heard that I had left the country after their arrest, so they blamed everything on me. They had agreed on a story among themselves and had all given the same testimony: they got the leaflets from a young woman named Lisa. Under duress, they gave a description of Lisa. She was a beautiful young woman whom they had not been able to resist. That alone would not have led the Gestapo to me, but all three of them were pressed for details and they made statements about dark curly hair, and freckles, and age and height, and who knows what else. At the hearing it appears that these three silly young boys were simply judged to be too young to comprehend the gravity of their actions. They had just played along for the excitement.

Indeed, they were soon released. And it was clear that they were now under surveillance.

I had to leave.

# BODENBACH

You have to get out of here," Bruno repeated. Karl also sent word that I had no time to waste. I was surprised to find my friends almost relieved that I was finally forced to go. It was very difficult for me. One less person.

They had my first name and a description. I had no place to stay, no papers. No money, no job. I knew that I couldn't hold out any longer.

Was I at greater risk because I was a Jew? Probably. Until now, however, it hadn't really been apparent. From time to time you could hear groups of Brownshirts growling out in unison one of their brilliant verses, for example:

*On to Jerusalem,*
*Stuff in the matzos, stuff in the matzos*
*Stuff in the matzos, stuff in the matzos*

But young SA recruits hawking *Angriff*, the Berlin Nazi daily, smiled at me flirtatiously, the same way they smiled at all the other girls. And I smiled back. We had all learned quickly, and it wasn't difficult when you understood why.

Bruno would come along and help me get across the border. He knew the Riesengebirge range better than I did. We had heard that it was not too difficult to go over the Schneekoppe, but we would have to check things out once we arrived in the area. Even if I was intending to cross the border illegally, I would have to have some kind of identification, made out in another name. Eva offered me her passport; later, she could report it lost and apply for a new one. And if something did go wrong, she could simply say it had been stolen. The description fit—brown hair, brown eyes, same height, same age—but the photo was useless. As an experiment I tried tweezing my eyebrows on one side, but it didn't work, Eva's face just wasn't my face. The photo would have to be replaced. Bruno said he

49

knew an expert forger who could take care of it for me. But of course there would be no exit visa.

It would only be for a short time. They hadn't gotten my full name from their prisoners; the boys hadn't known it, and it was possible that they'd just file this case away with the leaflets.

Anyway, how long could all this crap go on?

As it turned out, the only expert Bruno could dig up was no more than a petty thief from the Scheunenviertel, a poor quarter near the center of the city. He managed to replace the photo, but not without bending the rivet along the lower edge; if you looked closely enough you could see it had been pinched by some sort of pliers. I was not particularly comfortable with the thought of having to hand this passport over for inspection.

We had to change our plans. Bruno had broken his leg in a fall. There would be no hiking over the Schneekoppe; but he made it very clear that he did not want me to wait until his leg had healed. He had talked to his friend Heinz: Heinz would accompany me in Bruno's place.

I went to the location that Bruno and Heinz had agreed upon. But Heinz didn't show up. Arrested?

My cousin Anni returned from a second visit with my parents in Czechoslovakia. She said, "I'll go with you, we'll get through with my papers." Not a bad idea: not only the diplomatic passport, but the appropriate bearing as well—congenial, somewhat snobbish, elegant, a natural blond, as aryan as they come. I would not have expected this from Anni, it did after all require a lot of courage. And she had always insisted that she was "not in the least interested in politics."

But in the end, her plan also fell through. Andre was suddenly assigned to a post abroad and Anni had to go with him. Now I couldn't wait any longer; I would have to go alone. I knew that so many had already made it that it seemed to me I could succeed as well. If only that rivet on my passport photo didn't have such an amateur look!

Lucie helped me pack. "Good that you're finally getting out. It's about time. And I'll come to visit you in Prague."

I could only take a small suitcase with me, something easy to carry. For such a short time I wouldn't need all that much.

"Why are you packing that? I'll certainly be back before winter!" I said to Lucie. It was the heavy blue turtleneck sweater that my mother had knitted for me.

"It can get cold any time, and you don't know when you'll be back."
"You've got strange ideas."

Later, we are sitting together in my parents' apartment: Hans and Eva,
Bruno, Lucie, and I. It is a lovely apartment, but it isn't our home. Our
parents had moved here only a few months before, as quickly as they
could. That was at the very beginning of this Hitler business, when they
still believed we could survive the night falling over this country. Just get
away from Steglitz, where people knew our politics, move to another part
of the city! That's why they leased this apartment in Charlottenburg,
where no one knows us. In Charlottenburg! In the backyard of Storm-33,
the murdering storm troopers, the monsters of Berlin.

We go over everything once more, step by step. I will take the morning train to Prague. I will get off at the last stop before the Czech border.
From there I will find a way to get across.

Once I have gotten across the border I will go to Leitmeritz, a small
city north of Prague, to Uncle Robert's house where my parents are staying. They know I'll be coming soon. I sent them a postcard: "I'll be visit-
ing my uncle in a few days."

My brother goes to Anhalter Station with me. He asks the clerk,
"What's the German border station on the line to Prague?"

"Bodenbach."

"Bodenbach?" Hans asks. "Isn't that already Czechoslovakia?"

"Yes, but only once you leave the German zone inside the station."

"I see. One way to Bodenbach, please, first class."

We don't really know what this means for me. It will probably make
things easier. How often we've gone right through Bodenbach, but we
never had any reason to pay attention to the formalities of a border crossing. Right now we don't want to ask any more questions. I'll certainly be
able to get more information once I'm on the train. "Maybe you should
get out one station before Bodenbach," Hans suggests. "Or you can go as
far as Bodenbach and then take a local train back to the nearest German
town, and then you won't have to show your passport."

The train is quite empty. In my compartment there are two gentlemen traveling alone; they look like businessmen. I would like to start a
conversation because I think they probably know this route pretty well.
But it isn't very easy, I can't think of anything to say to them. Maybe they
could tell me something about the border.

One of them asks where I'm going. I want to spend a couple of days someplace nice, preferably in the mountains, I'm not really sure where. Maybe in the Erzgebirge or the Riesengebirge?

"From Bodenbach you can get a train to Schneidemühl," one of the gentlemen says.

"Or you can get off the train in Bad Schandau," the other suggests, "it's quite a pleasant area, too."

"Does the train stop anywhere between Bad Schandau and Bodenbach?" I ask.

"No, not the express."

That's right, this is an express. Now I remember: it goes directly from Bad Schandau to Bodenbach, without a stop.

I look out the window. Now comes the part of the trip I had always looked forward to: through the Saxon Alps. By the time we get to Bad Schandau, I will have to decide where I'm going to get out.

In Bad Schandau? It's too far from the border. In Bodenbach and then back a short way? That seems to be the most reasonable. In case anyone gives me any trouble there, all I have to do is tell the truth: I'm transferring to a local train here, I'm not crossing the border.

The train stops. Bad Schandau. No, it doesn't make any sense to get out here, what can I do here? I'll go as far as Bodenbach.

The train stops for a long time. I talk with the gentlemen in my compartment about various spas. I tell them I've decided on the Riesengebirge, it's so beautiful there.

The train leaves Bad Schandau.

Will our passports be checked before we get to Bodenbach? Of course, I can't really ask them that.

I had practiced Eva's signature until it was impossible to distinguish it from the signature in my passport. I know her personal statistics as well as I know my own.

Should I have gotten out? I don't know what's going to happen at the border. I should have thought it through more carefully, this may simply be stupid. . . . Now it's too late, the train's moving, and it won't stop until we get to Bodenbach.

Okay. I'm on the train to Bodenbach, and I'll get out and transfer there. A few days of vacation. My name is Eva Rosenthal. I was born on February 11, 1909, in Berlin. I live at 5 Bayrischer Platz, Berlin.

How long does it take to Bodenbach? I ask the two gentlemen. Only fifteen minutes more? Time has gone by so fast. That damned rivet at the bottom of my passport photo! And no exit visa. Now I'm getting nervous, but why? My name is Eva Rosenthal. . . .

Doors opening and closing, loud footsteps in the aisle. The two gentlemen take their suitcases down from the luggage rack; one of them hands me my bag. I thank him. "Pleased to be of help," he says. I want to ask if this is just a customs inspection or whether our passports will also be checked now; but no, I'd better not.

The door to our compartment slides open. There are three men in uniform, one of them in the uniform of a storm trooper.

"German border patrol. Your passports, please."

The two gentlemen hand over their passports, one after the other. I hold my passport in my hand. One of the customs officials reaches for it.

I give him my passport, and then I stand up and say: "I'm not crossing the border. I'm getting out here and transferring to a local train."

The customs official looks at me, then opens my passport and looks at my photo. Then he hands the passport to the storm trooper. He leafs through it. He looks at me carefully, his eyes shift back and forth between my face and the photo.

"Your name?" he asks, looking at the name in the passport.

Something cold, an icicle, runs through me from head to toe.

"My name is Eva Rosenthal."

I *am* Eva Rosenthal.

"Birthplace?"

"Berlin."

"Date?"

"February 11, 1909."

"Address?" His questions keep coming more quickly.

"5 Bayrischer Platz."

"City?"

"Berlin."

"Occupation?"

"Student."

The train stops.

He asks again, the same questions all over again, only in different order, very fast. Address? Birthdate? Occupation? Name? I answer, I don't make any mistakes—after all, I am Eva Rosenthal.

He looks at me again, very carefully. Then suddenly he hands me the passport. "Here. No, don't put it away. You're going to need it again. Get out and wait on the platform. Take your suitcase with you!" With his boot he kicks open the door to the platform. Turning around, I see the faces of the two gentlemen traveling with me, they're both staring at me, their jaws hanging open, their eyes full of fear. "Get out!" the storm trooper yells loudly from the open door.

I carry my bag and my passport in one hand, and steady myself with the other as I take the first step down to the platform. I can see there is another storm trooper standing on the platform directly below me. Astonished, and somewhat confused, he looks up at me. I slowly descend to the second step.

"Hurry up!"

That voice, but where's it coming from? "Come on, our train's leaving!"

The storm trooper standing below me turns his head in the direction of the voice. I step down onto the platform. A hand grabs my free arm and drags me a few steps. One shove and I stumble through a barrier. The voice says, "It's all right!" and the grip on my arm loosens.

"It's all right, we're in Czech territory now," the voice says.

Yes, it really is my father's voice.

I try to pull myself together. Let's go! Let's get away from this border, away from the SA! Where I'm out of their sight.

"You've crossed the border," my father says. "You are no longer in Germany. We're not on the run here."

"Won't they look for me here?"

"Once you're beyond the barrier, you're in Czechoslovakia. They can't come in and get you."

"The Brownshirt in the train noticed there was something wrong with my passport. He wanted to hold me."

"That's what I thought. When I heard his voice, the tone, I knew I had to do something."

"Yes, but how did you happen to be here?"

"We knew from your postcard that you would be coming one of these days. I figured you'd probably be taking the train to Bodenbach. So, just in case, I came and waited here, yesterday, and the day before yesterday too. From a spot near the barrier you can get a good view of the train from Berlin. But that's all over now and we're taking the train to Leitmeritz."

# LEITMERITZ

Mother and Toni were standing in front of the house.

"Look, they're waiting for us," my father said.

Toni was Uncle Robert's wife, but we didn't call her Aunt Toni, because she was too young to be an aunt. We had some difficulty communicating. Of course, here in the Sudetenland almost everyone spoke German, but Toni was from Prague and only spoke Czech, so my mother, or someone else in the family, had to interpret for us.

However, when I first arrived, my mother wanted to spend some time alone with me. She wanted me to tell her everything that had happened since we had last seen each other. She had to know what my brother was planning to do, how much longer he would be able to hold out, and when he would be leaving Germany.

"And what happened in Bodenbach?"

"Nothing much, really," I reported. "The storm trooper on the platform had simply heard the storm trooper on the train ordering me to 'Get out!' and when father suddenly yelled, in a very urgent voice, for me to hurry up, the Brownshirt became confused. By the time he understood what was happening, father had already pulled me over the border. What the storm trooper in the train might have said I can only imagine, but luckily I was already too far away to hear him."

"My God, you call that 'nothing much'? The risks you've been exposed to! Can you imagine how I've been trembling in fear for you these past few months?"

"No. No, you can't do that, you can't allow yourself to think like that. That's how we lead our lives over there—we push things like that out of our minds, everything that could keep us away from our work. Otherwise there wouldn't be anyone left with the strength to carry on."

That evening, after dinner, we sat together in the little garden behind the house. Uncle Robert, Toni, my parents, my cousin Fritz, me, and Wolf

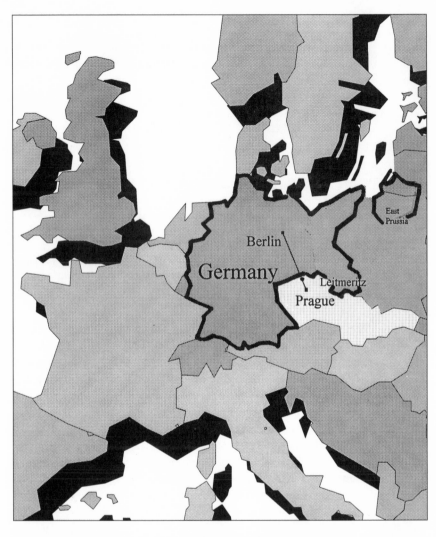

*Shortly after the Nazis took power, I was forced to flee Berlin. I escaped over the Czech border and stopped first in Leitmeritz. Then I went on to Prague, where I met Hans Fittko and we continued our resistance activities in exile.*

the dog. Just like the many times we had sat there before on our summertime visits to the Schaleks. And yet it was different. We weren't on vacation, we were refugees.

Even as a child I had always enjoyed spending my summers here in this small town. In my memory the sun was always shining here; very different from the gray and windy cities where I had grown up, and where it was usually raining. The streets, the houses, and the people seemed much friendlier. And then there was the Bohemian forest where my brother and I sometimes went hiking. Or we'd go to the swimming pool in the morning, and then, as long as the currents weren't too strong, we'd swim together across the Elbe, all the way to the other shore and back. But the grown-ups didn't have to know about this. Sometimes I'd get angry with my brother when he tried to force me to calculate the angle we had swum. Or sometimes we'd walk across the bridge and play for a while in the Theresienstadt fortress.

Now my mother asked, "Why don't you go swimming?"

"I don't really feel like it," I answered.

I read all the newspapers, looking for news from Germany. Sometimes arrests were reported. Then I'd try to figure out if it was someone I knew, and I imagined what would happen. Now, now that I was out I sometimes felt real panic. Now, for the first time, I was being hunted down, I was fleeing in my nightmares. I had no doubt that antifascist literature continued to be produced and distributed on the other side of the border. But here I was, in this lovely little town, cut off, without contact, and I no longer knew what was happening in Berlin. I would not stay here for very long.

"I thought you might be able to relax here," my mother said. But things didn't work out that way. The transition from the Terror in Berlin to this tranquillity had simply been too abrupt.

One evening a few days after my arrival we were sitting in the garden again. We were talking about the latest news from Germany, and, as always, the question that everyone asked here came up again: How could this be happening, especially in Germany? Uncle Robert said: "It could never happen here." Sometimes it almost sounded like a personal accusation: how could you let this happen?

We, let this happen? I thought. We're risking our lives.

Uncle Robert was talking about an article on the situation in Germany. He had read it in a highly respected newspaper, he said. I was surprised: if he really wanted to know what was happening over there, why didn't he ever ask me instead of reading a "highly respected newspaper"? And my thoughts again went out to the prisoners who were being tortured.

" . . . and Thälmann is a criminal!" I heard him say suddenly. "The Communists are the guilty ones."

"The victims are the guilty ones?" I shouted. "Fighting against the fascists is a crime? And that's what you, the chief magistrate, are saying?"

"Robert, you can't really believe that," my mother said.

He stood his ground. The Communists with their radical politics and demagoguery had frightened the good citizens. They had driven the Germans into the arms of the Nazis, whom they now saw as their saviors.

My father, who had said nothing until now, stood up. "Who'd like to go for a walk? We'll never agree about politics, so what's the use of arguing?"

No, I wouldn't stay here for long.

My father met an old acquaintance in the market square, Bruno Frei, who had previously been the editor-in-chief of *Berlin am Morgen*. Frei was just now working on a book about the Hanussen case. Hanussen was a pro-Nazi "seer" who had been murdered after the national socialist takeover, supposedly because he had "seen" too much. Frei had come to Leitmeritz to look up the chief trial judge and do an interview. "The chief judge is Robert Schalek," my father said, "my brother-in-law." He brought Frei home with him to meet Uncle Robert.

Bruno Frei had fled Berlin and was now living in Prague. He urged me to leave this "provincial nest" and talked about the large German emigré community in Prague. I would find that many of my friends who had fled Berlin were now staying there.

"And how would I support myself in Prague?" I wanted to know.

"Life isn't easy, but we manage," he said, and went on to describe emigrant life in a few words.

"Great," I said, "I'll be there. Soon."

# PRAGUE

Frei had given me the address of a reception center in Prague where emigrants were helped to find lodging for the first few nights.

I had expected to find an office, but instead it was an empty room in the basement of an apartment building. There were about a dozen people crowded together in this small room. Everything seemed very confused, people were talking at each other (at least it was in German!), but there was no one who could give me the information I needed. After a time, a young man came in and said that he had lodgings available. I gave him my name and he proceeded to ask me a series of questions. Where I had come from, why I had come to Prague, could I prove that I had been persecuted in Germany? My answers seemed to satisfy him, and he said all right. He had only wanted to be sure that I was not a Nazi agent. I had to laugh, and he laughed with me. "I know," he said, "what we're doing is a little childish, but there are so many people coming over that we really don't know what security measures we should be taking." He gave me a slip of paper with an address where I could find lodging for the night. It was a farmhouse outside the city, and he gave me directions how to get there by streetcar.

I was happy that the farmer's wife was able to speak a little German. She set out a plate of food for me—dumplings, just like the ones my mother always made. I was hungry. But before I could begin to eat, she wanted to know how such terrible things could be happening in Germany, such things would never happen here. The children—I believe there were three—sat around the kitchen table staring at me, and suddenly I had no answer, and the dumpling stuck in my throat. Then she said I should just relax and eat my dinner in peace. After I finished eating she took me to a room with a large double bed, and I knew immediately that it was their bedroom. I said to the wife: No, I can't take your bed, I'll just find some place in the kitchen, it's no problem for me. But she wouldn't hear of it, it just wouldn't do, I was after all her guest. I was too tired to argue any more. The woman put her arm around me and led me over to the huge bed, and I lay down. It was a warm night in July or August, and the bed was covered with a comforter thicker than any comforter I had ever seen. I didn't know whether I was supposed to sleep under it or on top of it. But before I could decide what to do, I somehow fell asleep and didn't wake up until the roosters crowed.

The first thing I wanted to do was look up Aunt Emma, my father's sister, who was living in Prague. I took the streetcar back into the city, and at the stop where I transferred I saw a group of young people: they weren't Czechs, and they weren't tourists either. Definitely German emigrants. One of them looked very familiar, his name was Herbert; and there was another one, Emil. I had met both of them in Berlin working with the Antifa, a group formed to resist the growing fascist threat. Wherever I went in Prague I met up with emigrants! We greeted one another with great enthusiasm, and Herbert said: "We are so happy that you got out! We have to celebrate."

I was confused. "Happy? Why? And what do you want to celebrate?"

"That another one of us has escaped! We always celebrate when someone gets out."

"One more here—that means one fewer over there. How can we celebrate that?" I asked.

No, they didn't see things that way. It was important to save as many people as possible now. We seemed to be in disagreement on this point. Do we all change so quickly when we become emigrants? I asked myself. At any rate, the two of them gave me several addresses and lots of advice about how to survive as an emigrant.

Emma Marek was a widow; she had a large apartment. I could, if necessary, spend a few nights there, she said, but I shouldn't think of it as a permanent arrangement: she had a number of tenants already. What's more, our Uncle Julius, as well as our cousin George, had recently fled Berlin and were also staying with her. She just didn't have another bed available.

Then there was my cousin Eileen and her family. When Aunt Emma called to tell her about my arrival, she asked Aunt Emma to tell me that she was very sorry, she would dearly love to help me and the other members of our family who had fled, but just now it was not possible because she badly needed a new fur coat. George and I started to laugh; we simply couldn't stop laughing, and Aunt Emma scolded us for being so silly: she didn't think it was funny at all; it was appalling. For the time being I left my suitcase there, the one I had been dragging around with me, and went to a soup kitchen near Wenceslaus Square, where, according to my fellow emigrants, midday meals were served to refugees.

That day it was potato soup. There I met a lot of people from Berlin, a few of them acquaintances, and they all had hundreds of questions. You could hear many others speaking with a strong Saxon accent—for the people who had to flee Saxony, the Czech border was the closest. They were all ready to give me advice, especially the "old emigrants" who had arrived here some days before. I was most interested in finding out where they all lived. For example, there was a dormitory in Vodičkova, but it was only for men. Most of the women had been helped to find lodgings by various committees. Being a Jew, I should first look to the Jewish Committee. And then I would have to register with the police and get my papers in order.

Two young emigrants accompanied me. They wanted to help me get settled and had nothing better to do. The police station was packed with emigrants who were waiting for their papers. I got in the line for new emigrants and was given a form to fill out. I sat down on a bench and was about to begin, when I saw that I had four pages full of questions in Czech, and of course I could not understand a word. How was I to answer questions I didn't understand? I knew that since the end of the Hapsburg monarchy, officials here often refused to speak German, even if it was their native language. The monarchy, for its part, had repressed the Czechs and their language, put them down, and treated them as second-class citizens. But what good was this historical insight to me? It was of very little help in filling out a Czech questionnaire. I hesitated and, since my new friends had disappeared, finally went back to the window and explained to the clerk that I couldn't understand the questions. Might he be able to help me? He looked at me and said, in perfect German, without blinking an eye, "*Ich spreche nicht deutsch.*"

"Please tell me what I should do! I really do not understand a single word of Czech," I said.

"When I go to Germany," he said, "will your police officials speak to me in Czech? Do you think they'll give me a questionnaire in Czech?"

"They are not *my* police," I said and stared at him angrily. "I am a refugee." And since I had already built up a head of steam, I added: "Are you planning to spend your vacation in the Third Reich? I hope you enjoy yourself!"

He looked me over again, from head to toe, grew rather embarrassed, and said, "Back there!" pointing to a man sitting behind a desk. The man helped me fill out the form. Apparently he had been assigned there expressly for this purpose, and the clerk at the window had simply found it amusing to make my life a little more difficult. When I had finally finished and handed the signed document back to him, he said I should come back in a week to pick up my interim passport. "Interim passport," what a strange term; I'had never heard it before. A passport for an interim life; it was somehow appropriate. We lived a very interim existence here; but now I would at least have a genuine passport, I would be Lisa Ekstein again, and I could be legally registered with the police. Interim? That means: until we can go back home.

In the meantime both of my escorts had reappeared. They explained that the emigrants had found a way around the crazy language barrier within the bureaucracy. Bureaucrats and police were required to speak French with foreigners who spoke no Czech. Since only a very few of them could speak French, all you had to do was ask them, *"Parlez-vous français?"* and they immediately began speaking German.

I spent the night at Aunt Emma's. With her perfect posture and dark hair you couldn't tell that she was in her seventies, and she kept her age an absolute secret. In the family she was known as "Aunt Emma the Younger," because we also had an "Aunt Emma the Elder," who was well past eighty. George surprised me: he offered me his bed and slept on a small sofa, which really was a sacrifice considering the fact that his long legs hardly fit into a full-size bed. The next day I began looking for an organization that could help me settle in.

First, the Jewish Committee. By coincidence, the director, Frau Dr. Schmolka, was also a niece of Aunt Emma the Elder, but from the other side of the family. Our mutual aunt had written to Mařka Schmolka and told her that I was a political emigrant and had worked in the resistance against the Nazis. She had asked Mařka to please take good care of me. But I didn't hear about this until later.

The waiting room, with its bare white walls, was full of people. The few chairs were occupied, and after signing in I sat down on a window sill. A man approached me. He was from Berlin and said he had recognized me immediately—by my legs. I saw a few more familiar faces. We waited hour after hour, we had plenty of time to talk: that's the way it was, that's the way it is now, what will happen next? Escape. Life there, and how each of us, in his own way, was trying to get on with it. We talked about Prague and how different things were here, and a few of the emigrants were ready, then and there, to take me on a tour of the Old Town. But I already knew Prague; my mother had often taken me to visit her hometown and had not only shown me the Pulverturm, the Veits Cathedral, and the Town Hall, but also where she had lived as a child, and where my grandfather had had his bookstore.

But now—this was no longer the same city. It was foreign to us refugees.

It was still a wonderful city, in the opinion of others sitting in the waiting room.

"That may be," said a young man, "but the bedbugs! Everywhere they send us to stay there are bedbugs crawling up and down the walls. At least we don't have bedbugs like that in Germany."

"Yes, but here there are friendly people."

"But how many of them speak German?"

"And the sausages, the ones they call *Würschtln*—they're delicious. We don't have anything nearly as good."

"Right, with horseradish. But it tastes a little different here and they call it *Kren*."

Homesick? I thought. Homesick for horseradish, homesick for our own familiar language.

I wasn't called in until the next day. The Jewish Committee gave out lodging coupons to all of us whose cases they had not been able to complete. I spent the night with several other emigrants at the home of a Frau Taussig in the city center.

The next day new emigrants came. We waited, we talked. Late in the afternoon Frau Schmolka had me called into her office. We had never met before, and I hadn't really heard much about her from my family. When someone did mention her, one or the other would say: "Maťka is so competent, she really is." Other than that, I didn't know a thing about her.

She told me that our mutual Aunt Emma had already announced my visit. She understood that I was at risk because of my illegal activities, apparently in connection with left-leaning political groups. I was therefore considered a political refugee, and the Jewish Committee did not support political refugees.

"Even if they are Jews?"

"Not when they have fled for political reasons."

"Your committee doesn't help Jews who have fought against the Hitler regime?"

"It is not our responsibility."

"In that case, whom do you support?" I asked.

"Only nonpolitical Jewish refugees," she answered. "Only people who have had to flee because they are Jews. There are agencies for intellectuals, for writers, for artists, for political activists—you'll have to find another committee."

Apparently she had decided from the very beginning to get rid of me as soon as possible. Why? I didn't know if those really were committee rules or merely her interpretation of them. In any case, there was no point in continuing our conversation. She is so competent, Marka really is, I thought. Maybe competent people should not be put in charge of refugee-aid committees.

On my way out I warned my acquaintances in the waiting room: "Do not admit to any 'political involvement.'" Then, as I had been advised, I went to the Grossmann Committee.

There were very few people in the waiting room, all of them men. A few looked familiar. But it was possible that I had seen them in pictures, or that they reminded me of the regulars at the Romanischen Café. They were better dressed than the people in the waiting rooms of the other committees, but you could see that they were beginning to lose ground, as is always the case—cuffs a bit worn, collars not really dirty but not clean either, no one clean-shaven. They sat there quietly, kept to themselves, had nothing to say to one another or simply no desire to speak. Feeling that I didn't really belong here, I also kept quiet. After a few hours I was called into Kurt Grossmann's office. I had met him once, through my father. I had come to the wrong place, he said. His committee worked solely with well-known authors, famous artists, and other distinguished intellectuals. Since I enjoyed no renown at all, I left.

A young woman whom I knew from the Office Workers' Union advised me to go to the Czech unions. They had helped her.

It worked. The Czechs gave tickets to union members who had fled Germany. The tickets were good for one meal a day at the union cafeteria, and we were also given a small sum of money to help cover the cost of our lodging. After this, my emigrant's life began to look up.

Someone showed me an ad for a furnished room in the city center, and it appeared to be cheap enough even for my budget. The landlady was friendly and spoke German. However, the furnished room was a surprise. It was clean, but the furnishings consisted of three beds and a wash basin. I gave the woman a questioning look, and she explained:

"Yes, I thought you might like to have some company."

It so happened that two long-time acquaintances, charming young ladies, had just arrived in Prague. They both worked and would not disturb me during the day. And at night, we all slept anyway.

At the moment I have no other choice, I said to myself. We are emigrants, after all. And this is just an interim arrangement.

I almost never saw one of my roommates. She left early and returned late. The second was a lovely blond girl, very young, and we smiled at each other, but beyond that we were not really able to communicate. On Sundays a collapsible bathtub was set up in the kitchen, water was heated, and the family and tenants bathed, one after the other. This isn't exactly a luxury hotel, I thought, but I'll get used to it.

After about a week, early one morning, while the blond and I were still sleeping, there was a loud noise outside our room, and then a vigorous knock on the door, as if from a giant fist. Someone pulled on the door and forced it open. A large, fat woman appeared in the doorway and threw herself on the beautiful young girl asleep in her bed. The girl leapt up, and the two of them yelled at each other, and the fat woman shook both her fists in the air. I didn't understand a word, but it was still very exciting. The young girl ran around the room in circles and screeched, catching her breath from time to time, and the old one was on her heels, howling.

I quickly threw on some clothes and went into the kitchen, where I found our landlady standing with her hands over her ears. The scandal had become quite unpleasant for me, still I wanted to know what was wrong. It was a remarkable experience to be part of a scene like this without understanding what was happening.

My landlady explained everything in detail. The fat woman's son was studying in Prague, or, more to the point, was supposed to be studying in Prague. The young girl had followed him here from their hometown in the provinces, and the young man had said he was going to give up his studies and marry her. His mother threatened to have the girl arrested and put in prison if she didn't break off the relationship and leave Prague immediately. She honored the girl with a string of titles that my landlady repeated in Czech but declined to translate. The girl adamantly refused to give up the student because she loved him, and thus the loud screams.

Maybe I should look for another place to sleep.

# Emigrant Housing

Sometimes I went to eat at the soup kitchen and gave away my meal ticket for the union cafeteria, where the meals were better and more substantial. It was a welcome change. I always met friends at the soup kitchen; and there were new arrivals, the political refugees. From them you could find out what was going on over there: the illegal resistance work, the persecutions, the escapes.

For many of the visitors to the soup kitchen, their noonday meal was all they had to eat, and they received no other aid. Mostly they were workers who had never been abroad before. They had had to flee: they were antifascists; they were being hunted down by the Nazis. . . . If they were caught, they would be murdered.

Very few of the emigrants with big names came to the soup kitchen. They were able to find support (usually quite meager) elsewhere. They had also been forced to flee, and had fought fascism with their own weapons. They would have been killed too.

A few of my friends at the soup kitchen told me they were planning to rent a cheap apartment together. Did I want to join them? As a group, with the help of one or another committee, it would be possible. I thought: even if it's a bit crowded, it will be better than the endless moving and searching for a place to stay. There was a development of new apartment buildings just outside the city, and we went to talk to the management. That area was called Krč. We tried to pronounce Krč correctly, but it wasn't easy, twisting our tongues, hissing and gurgling, without spitting. It sounded more or less like *kertsch*, or *kretsch*. The Czechs laughed at us.

The apartment consisted of one large room, a tiny kitchen, and a small bathroom with modern conveniences. I was especially fortunate to be assigned the kitchen, where there was a small, child-size sofa next to the gas stove. Of course, the sofa was quite narrow, but it was large enough for me. For a few weeks I even shared it with Eva when she came from Berlin for a visit. We got the sofa from Czechs who wanted to help us emigrants. People came from time to time and brought pieces of furniture, blankets, or pots and pans; sometimes they even brought food. They said they had heard about us through friends.

In the large room there were five beds lined up one next to the other. The sleepers often changed. It was city housing, comfortably middle-class, but the rents were cheap and we all chipped in whenever we could. On the ground floor there was even a laundry with washing machines, a luxury almost unknown at the time.

After a while I was able to find some hourly work, but that was unusual. I had been given the address of a woman who was writing a book in German and needed someone to type the manuscript. It was a novel, and every day she wrote out several pages, which I then typed on her small typewriter. It was supposed to be the dramatic love story of a baron and an actress, and when the author was uncertain about her plot, she asked my advice: would it be better if the baron turned out to be a rogue, or maybe the actress should be a loose woman? I didn't really know much about novels like this and suggested that it might be interesting if, this time, both of them turned out to be rotten scoundrels. She didn't accept my suggestion; supposedly it offended her innermost sensibilities.

Every morning, she had her maid bring me a cup of tea and a sandwich. Once we had a lot to do, so she asked me to stay longer and invited me to lunch, where I met her family. They started talking about someone I had met through Uncle Robert. When I mentioned this, the author looked at me, astonished. "Good God, if you are Judge Schalek's niece, who is your mother?"

"I am his sister's daughter," I said, "Julie's daughter."

As it turned out, the novelist had gone to school with my mother in Prague, and she described my mother's schoolbag, light-brown leather trimmed in black, and she then confessed to having pushed my mother down the steps, out of envy. From then on, I got two sandwiches every morning. That was very nice, because I was always hungry—we were all hungry, all the time.

One day a man named Jiři showed up more or less out of the blue. He wanted to make a small donation to help an emigrant with the cost of food. Lenchen, a very young girl from Berlin, and I had been chosen to receive this aid, maybe because we were the skinniest. We were introduced to Mr. Jiři, and Mr. Jiři immediately took it upon himself to fatten the two of us up. Jiři was a stout man, about forty years old. Lenchen and I started meeting him in the city every Wednesday. We went shopping, bought lots of fruit and the wonderful Prague ham that almost melts on your tongue. What a remarkable change from our usual diet of bread and Reklami salami, the only meat we could afford on our own! But above all, I will forever remember Jiři for the fruit crème he always bought us for dessert.

Sometimes I took my purchases to the Vodičkova dormitory. I shared Jiři's presents with a group of friends, and together we prepared wonderful dinners. After dinner, the residents, as well as any guests who might happen to be there, often began to sing. We sang the antifascist songs we had sung over there; and sometimes even a few schmalzy folk songs that we had always made fun of before. Disabled veterans and jobless people used to sing these songs in the backyards of Berlin and hope that, from some window, someone would throw them a Sechser, a five-pfennig piece, wrapped in newspaper. One of these songs, "Krug zum grünen Kranze," was about a wanderer who came to an inn, where his dear old mother saw him and immediately recognized who he was. Another was about a little flower, the title was "Forget-Me-Not," and then there was "O My Dear Edelweiss, a Thousand Greetings to You!" And the two birch trees, with the three gypsies in the meadow, we sang that one, too. And the dark brown maid, *hollerie und hollera*. All about home. I don't know how we got around to the Volga Boat Song, probably because it makes everyone feel so nostalgic—when Stjenka Rasin throws his dearest overboard into the angry current, and the Volga carries her away. I noticed one of the newcomers. His name was Hans; he had a beautiful voice.

When I left Berlin, Lucie and Käthe had promised to visit me in Prague. I had been waiting for them all this time, but I could hardly believe it when they actually showed up! They had dressed up as hikers and smuggled themselves in across the Riesengebirge. When they told me about our friends, I was shocked to hear how many had been arrested. Even Bruno had been arrested, then soon let go. But now he was under surveillance and had to keep his distance from everyone. Käthe told me how she had asked my brother to marry her—a marriage of convenience, of course—so she could get an Austrian passport and emigrate legally. But he had turned her down in no uncertain terms because he and Eva were planning to marry soon and emigrate to France.

Käthe and Lucie wanted to relax in Prague. But it was impossible. Maybe it really would be better to go hiking in the mountains? So they went off and I stayed behind. For the first time in all these years something seemed to be separating us. I would never have imagined it, but I just could not spend a vacation with them, knowing that they would return to the Third Reich and I would stay behind, an emigrant in a neighboring country.

The nightmares came back. Always exactly the same dream. I could not understand why it was always on the Möckern Bridge where they hunted me down in my dreams, where they grabbed for me, where I suffered in terror. . . . This is it, the end; I sensed it in my dream; it was inescapable. When I woke up, I couldn't remember anything like this that had really taken place on the Möckern Bridge.

It was impossible to forget anything in Prague. There were so many who were so young and had turned old in SA cellars and Gestapo jails. Sometimes I took sick people to Czech doctors who had offered to help us. I went to the clinic with one young man and told one of the doctors I knew: since escaping the torture chamber this young man has blood in his urine. I saw the anger in the doctor's eyes. I asked him: you take care of sick people all day—why is it that our patients affect you like this?

"I am sickened, I am horrified, when I see what people over there are capable of doing to their fellow human beings," he said.

In the meantime my parents had moved on to Vienna. Relatives had invited them to stay for a time. My father tried to renew old business contacts outside of Germany. When he had decided simply to leave everything behind in Germany and give up his position with the export company, he had been assured: for you, dear Mr. Ekstein, there will always be a place at one of our branch offices abroad. But the London branch he had worked with so often, after a lot of talk back and forth, finally said: under current circumstances, a continuing association with you would simply not be feasible; they were a German company after all. . . . He received lots of replies like that. His earlier connections did him no good at all. They were completely erased, as if they had never existed. He kept looking.

I saved enough money from my work as a typist to buy a train ticket and spend a few days in Vienna. There I noticed that my father had changed, had become introverted. His optimism, which had never deserted him before, seemed to be cracking. I supposed it had to happen.

I was surprised that my mother, in spite of everything, despite all her worries, had not changed. Maybe it was because she had always been more realistic. Normal life had broken down completely, but she had not broken down.

Before I had a permanent address in Krč, I had given my parents and a few friends the address of the Vodičkova dormitory. It was in the middle of the city, a few steps from Wenceslaus Square, and I dropped by every few days to check on my mail. One day I went there again and asked Willi, the "postman," if he had anything for me. He said he wasn't distributing the mail anymore, I should ask Hans, the new arrival from Berlin. Hans, who actually had a letter for me, had caught my attention a couple of times, and not just because of his singing voice. He was quite different from most of the people here. In what way? He was levelheaded and always calm. I had noticed that when there were arguments among the residents—tempers were often short—Hans was the one to whom people came for advice. He often found an answer, and people seemed to listen to him, probably because he was so levelheaded. We talked for a while, and I thought he was rather nice. His name was Hans Fittko and he was from Spandau.

*Hans Fittko, Berlin-Spandau, 1932*

# BORDER WORK

Edith Kahn knocked on the door that separated my sleeping kitchen from the *pavlač*. The *pavlač* is a corridor that runs along the outside of the building like a long, narrow balcony, and Edith and Otto Kahn lived with their two little girls on the same floor we did, at the other end of the *pavlač*. "Heinz will be coming by in a while," Edith said. "He's bringing a young friend with him. Would you like to come over, too? You know, it's Christmas Eve, and my sister baked a cake."

The Kahns were friendly people. We talked, as we always did, about reports from Germany, and how long all this might last. Heinz had brought a bottle of wine; he didn't want to say where he'd got it. In the dormitory outside of Prague, where Heinz and his friend Herbert lived, there were a number of young Jews who were training for a profession, preparing themselves to leave for Palestine. After dinner, both children were put to bed and we all withdrew into the kitchen and sat around the table continuing to talk about "whisper propaganda" and its effect on the Nazi campaign against the "whiners and trouble-makers." We told each other the latest jokes from over there: about Goebbels, who was called "Wotan's Mickey Mouse" or "the man with the fiery tongue," to whom Goetz was said to have replied, "Fiery or not, you can still kiss my . . . !" and the latest fat-Göring lampoon, "Tinsel Hermann," showing the many medals hanging over his belly: "Tinsel left, tinsel right, still the fool's too fat to fight . . . !"

There was lots to laugh about. Herbert, the young man Heinz had brought with him from the dormitory, was only seventeen or eighteen and rather shy, but he joined in the general banter. We also played a kind of pawn-shop game, although there wasn't much to be put in play. I wanted Heinz's black beret; but he refused, saying, in all earnestness, that he would never be parted from the hat, not ever in his life. We all thought this was a little silly, and we laughed. I wanted to know how his plans for emigration to Palestine were coming along, and Heinz said that he was going, everything was ready. I asked him if he was a Zionist, and he said, no, definitely not, but the two of them had no other choice, it was impossible for them to get along on their own without the free food and shelter they were getting. And how long would all this last, and then what? Anyway, there were opportunities to build socialism in Palestine, I should know that. I hadn't meant to upset Heinz by my question, but it seemed to have annoyed him.

It had gotten late and I wanted to go home. Edith said that Heinz and Herbert had probably missed the last streetcar but could stay overnight with them. She and her husband slept with the children in the main room; Heinz and Herbert could sleep in the kitchen. Heinz thought it would be simpler if Herbert went back with me to my apartment and slept in my kitchen, where there was just as much room as there was at the Kahns'. I said: What a strange idea! I have to sleep in the kitchen, too. Herbert said, somewhat embarrassed: It doesn't matter to me, however you want to work it out. Heinz kept insisting, and I said no, out of the question. Then Heinz started to complain and insisted that I ought to be willing to do him this small favor: he always had to sleep in a cavernous hall with twenty-five other people, and now, for once, when he had a chance to sleep alone in a room, I was going to spoil it for him.

It got to be too much, so I stood up, saying I was tired, and went back along the *pavlač* to my apartment, shaking my head.

In the morning I was awakened by a loud noise. Someone was knocking on my kitchen door. A couple of my roommates got up drowsily and came out to see what was happening. I opened the door to the *pavlač*. One of the neighbors, who spoke German, said, breathlessly, "He turned on the gas." She pointed toward the Kahn apartment.

"Who?" I asked. "Where are they?" I saw the police coming out of the Kahns' apartment and I ran to their door. Someone held me back.

"No, you're not going in there."

I was pulled back to my kitchen. "What happened? Where are the children?"

"The family's okay . . . the youngest child screamed and woke her parents. Both young men . . . no, don't go in there. The corpses will be picked up right away."

The corpses. Two young men in Prague . . . from Germany . . . two corpses. Heinz had not wanted to take the innocent young Herbert with him on his final emigration, but when his plan didn't work, that is just what happened. He had endangered the entire family, including the children. In Prague the cooking gas is odorless, and it must certainly have leaked through the kitchen door into the main room. What a strong desire for death he must have had!

Why?

It was irrelevant now, but I kept asking myself: Why couldn't he part with his black beret, even up to his death?

In the evening, we often met in the Café Kontinental on Národni Avenue. You could sit at our table for an entire evening with a cup of coffee or a cappuccino, and the waiters, who knew us, would continue to bring us water, and even newspapers. We sat there and talked, sometimes late into the night. We always discussed what was happening over there: the politics of the leftist parties, and how best to carry on the struggle against fascism.

Once we got to know each other better, Hans Fittko persuaded me again and again to spend the evening with him at the Café Kontinental. Many of the emigrés who were regulars there had known him through his work with Franz Pfemfert and the publication *Aktion*. Through Pfemfert, who had published an anthology of contemporary Czech poetry, he knew several Czech journalists and authors. There was Grete Reiner, her sparkling dark eyes lined in black, who had translated Hašek's *The Good Soldier Schweyk* into German. Why did Grete always show up everywhere he was? I asked Hans. I was just imagining things, he replied, she was nothing more than an acquaintance, an older woman. Oh, I see, I said.

Then there were the Ottwalts, who came to the Kontinental almost every evening. Ernst was a lawyer and author of the well-known book *For They Know What They Are Doing*. His wife, Traute, came from a minister's family, it was obvious, you just sensed it in her bearing. You could also see how hard she was trying to fit into this milieu and the bohemian ways of her husband.

Sometimes, well-known writers and artists stopped by here on their way through Prague. They never talked about where they were going, and no one asked.

Johnny Heartfield came and stayed a while. From the Kontinental he wanted to go on to a wine bar, someplace where you could dance. We were rather surprised that he was so interested in finding a place to dance, but finally decided to go with him to a club we knew. There were about a dozen of us crowded together in a very small room, perspiring. Johnny ordered a few bottles of wine and paid. Then he wanted to dance, but no one else really felt like it. "Okay," Johnny said. "Then I'll do a dance for you." We formed a circle around him. He stood in the middle and turned his cap around, beak to the back.

"It's a sailors' dance," he said, "a real one that only sailors can do. That's where I learned it, from sailors."

He slipped something to the musicians and they started to play. It was a medley of all kinds of music—gypsy songs, tangos and waltzes and csardas—and Johnny danced. Skinny as he was, he leapt around stiffly, waving his arms, his legs, and his head, just like some life-size jumping jack. His face was a mask: pale, immobile, deadly serious. We all clapped our hands and he kept leaping, faster and faster, his sprawling legs looking for all the world like chopsticks. Johnny's dance was a spectacular success, but I found it somewhat discomforting; what could be going on in his mind? I had never seen him like this before.

He never showed up again. Where had he gone? To Moscow? Paris? Or maybe America?

In Prague at this time, people were very friendly and helpful toward emigrants. They shook their heads and wondered how it could possibly be that we—the Germans—had allowed the national socialists to come to power. "That could never happen here!" we kept hearing. But they did want to help us; they sensed that life here, far from our homes, must be difficult. Movie theaters gave out free tickets through the committees, and we were often invited into concerts and theater performances.

Hans wanted me to go with him to every last concert, and he was a dedicated moviegoer. We got to know the artistry of actors like Voskovec and Werich. What they did on stage was something completely new for us! It was also wonderful to see and hear it together with Hans, and to talk about it.

Hans was a night owl, and on those evenings, even when it got to be late, he still wanted to go to the Kontinental and talk with his friends. He needed people. And people needed him. All kinds of people.

It occurred to me that Willi, the "postman" at the Vodičkova, was distributing the mail again. "Didn't you say you'd taken on that job?" I asked Hans.

"Yes, but only for a short time."

"How short?"

"A few days."

"Interesting. That doesn't really seem to make much sense. Tell me the truth!"

"Okay. Until you picked up your mail, and I got a chance to meet you."

"So you were just putting on an act!"

"If it's for love, that doesn't count as pretense."

Hans often came out to Krč, but there were times when he stayed away for days and I didn't hear a thing from him. He had told me about his escape from Germany. In Berlin, Franz Pfemfert's brother-in-law, Heinrich Schäfer, had put him in contact with ski instructors who were familiar with the slopes near the Czech border. Things didn't go as smoothly as had been hoped: Hans had missed the first rendezvous point—he had lost his way but was able belatedly to find the fallback site, a ski cabin, where he had to wait several days until contact with his border guide could be reestablished and they could start. Shortly before they were to cross the border, they heard something, and then saw what it was, an SA patrol marching in their direction. His guide pointed to the right, toward a nearby stand of trees. An abrupt and daring dash through the forest, and they were on Czech soil.

From Prague, Hans had again taken up contact with his border guides. They were Friends of Nature, a socialist group, who were willing to help lead refugees over the border. They also took our anti-Nazi literature over the border into Germany. And that's why Hans sometimes disappeared from Prague, as he explained. He went to the border to cultivate these contacts.

Along with other political refugees, we were putting together material, writing flyers and brochures. Hans had friends among various Czech cooperatives, and they helped with printing and duplication.

Finally, I was able to help again. I could again do something to contribute to the downfall of the regime of horrors: I wrote, typed, and sometimes even went to the border to deliver materials to our contacts. I picked up people whom the guides had brought across. I was able to help!

My cousin Fritz often came to Prague and visited me in Krc. He was studying to be a tanner at a trade school in Freiberg, Saxony, so he was traveling back and forth between Czechoslovakia and Germany rather often. When I asked him, he answered me immediately, "Yes, I can carry letters for you across the border and mail them in Germany."

(When we met again in Prague in 1986, fifty years had passed. I asked Fritz about what he had done with the letters; I could only remember it vaguely. "Of course, I didn't ask anything about the contents of the letters back then," he said, "and I still don't know what was in those envelopes;

but it was very clear to me that I was carrying illegal material. You can't know how happy and how proud I was to be taking part in the struggle against the Nazi regime! There was no address on the envelopes when I took them across the border. You had me memorize the address and write it on the envelope once I had gotten into Germany. You were adamant! And I repeated this address over and over again to myself, and I've never forgotten it. I still know it: the name was 'Drucker,' it was in Wannsee, Waltharistrasse 11b." I searched and searched my memory, but I just couldn't think of who got those letters. I had discarded them as so much useless ballast, the way we always did with names and addresses: what I don't know won't hurt me. Today, I would dearly love to know who Drucker on Waltharistrasse was.)

In the meantime, Hans had moved out of the Vodičkova dormitory and was living with Czech friends. One day the police came to the apartment and arrested him.

A Gestapo spy had managed to infiltrate our group of border contacts. He told the Czech authorities everything he knew about activities there, the movement of fugitives into Czechoslovakia, the transport of antifascist literature into Germany, and the people who were organizing these activities. And that is how the Czech authorities had come to know the name and whereabouts of one Johannes Fittko.

The friend in whose apartment Hans was arrested was named Petr. He belonged to one of the cooperatives Hans was working with. Petr told his organization about the arrest, and they immediately sent a delegation to the authorities. In response to their inquiry, the police said that the arrest had been made because a German by the name of Fittko, a foreigner, had become involved in the domestic affairs of Czechoslovakia. The delegation from the cooperative threatened a mass protest if the prisoner were not set free by six o'clock that evening. The Czech authorities agreed to let him go on one condition, that Fittko, upon his release, leave the country without delay; he was to be banned from Czechoslovakia for life. On what grounds? He had, through his illegal activities, jeopardized the good relations between Czechoslovakia and the German Reich.

That same evening, after his release, Hans went directly to Reichenberg, a city north of Prague. Petr passed this information along to me, but I heard nothing from Hans for more than two weeks. Then one day Petr told me to be in a small wine cellar around ten o'clock in the evening. Did this mean that Hans was back in Prague?

Yes, Hans was sitting in the wine cellar, it was really him, even though his looks had changed considerably. He had grown a mustache, his black hair was a steely gray, cut short and parted.

"No one would know you, but still . . . what if they catch you here?"

"I couldn't leave right away. First we had to be sure that the communications between Prague and the border were kept up," he said. "The land of Thomas Masaryk has banned me for life because I refuse to give up the fight against fascism. A poor country, that believes it can't happen here."

"And what's going to happen now?"

"Over these past few days, I've been able to contact friends in Switzerland. They send literature into Germany on a regular basis. So, we're going to Basel."

"*We* are going to Basel, did you say?"

"Yes. I'll go first, and you can join me as soon as I've gotten settled."

"And when will that be?"

"Soon, very soon. Don't you know how much I missed you while I was waiting for this mustache to grow?"

# FROM PRAGUE TO BASEL

Our interim passports were only valid inside Czechoslovakia. If you are banned from a country you have to leave. But how do you leave without travel documents?

With a valid German passport you can enter Switzerland without a visa. But we emigrants, most of whom had come over the border illegally, didn't have German passports. Besides, having permission to enter a country is a far cry from having permission to reside there. Residence permits were hard to get in Switzerland: either you had to have a fat bank account or a big name, best of all both—like Thomas Mann, for example. But the majority of political refugees from Germany who had fled across the border into Switzerland had neither, so were forced to live there illegally.

In Prague, Hans got a pair of glasses, a hat, and a long tie to replace his bow tie. Then he took care of securing communications between Prague and our contacts along the border. He almost never showed himself in the city. Czech friends sheltered him while he finished his work. A rabbi who had befriended Hans married us in a quick ceremony, or, to be more precise, issued us a marriage certificate, when we explained the situation to him. (I am not certain what was written on the certificate, because, like most of our other papers, it was lost during the war while we were constantly on the run.) I can remember thinking back then: we can never know when we might need this kind of identification. At the time, all it did was make me the wife of a man who had been exiled for life.

Hans didn't have a passport. Old friends who were living in Basel would help him over the border. He said he had papers that would get him to the Swiss border. I don't remember what kind of papers those were.

I did have a valid German passport, not in my name but in the name of Eva Rosenthal, with a bent rivet on the lower edge of the photo. But I also had a real passport, my own Austrian document, and Austrians did

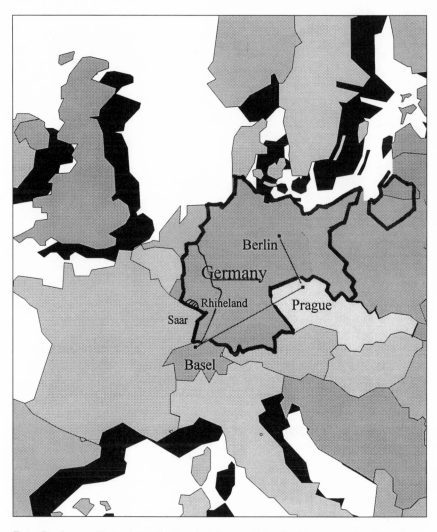

*From Basel we could clearly see the direction Nazi ambitions had begun to take. The industrial Saar region was reabsorbed in 1935. The Rhineland was remilitarized in 1936, and German factories were engaged in secret and illegal arms production.*

not need a visa to enter Switzerland. Of course, I had not brought it with me across the border into Czechoslovakia. In the meantime, however, my brother had been sending it to me page by page: one page with each letter, and finally the cover too. It had all arrived in good order and I had only to reassemble it—very carefully and very precisely, of course. This passport, my own genuine passport, would get me into Switzerland.

"Good. Everything's set," said Hans. "I've got to get out of here. And you'll be joining me soon!"

Everything had happened so fast, and I was so startled, that I had hardly had a moment to collect my thoughts. Not that there was any doubt: I wanted to follow him, I wanted to be with him. But it was also very clear that these past few weeks had been nothing more than a taste of what was to come in Hans Fittko's life. And my life would be a part of his.

As soon as Hans had left, I started waiting for news of his safe arrival in Basel. I wandered through the streets of Prague thinking: What is life like in Basel, how can we get by as illegal emigrants? Life isn't exactly easy here, but we manage. There will be many things I'll miss when I'm in Basel. At a corner I came upon a group of street singers with an accordion, and, as always, I stopped and listened, I just couldn't tear myself away from this music. Would there be street singers in Basel? Certainly they would play different melodies from the Slavic ones that accompanied us everywhere we went here in Prague. And in Switzerland, everything's supposed to be almost unbearably clean. . . .

I went home to Krč. We had moved into a larger apartment where we had two big rooms, each with two rows of beds, and we were able to shelter more emigrants. Anne and Berta were at home. They were both from small towns in Saxony and had both lost their husbands to the Nazi Terror, but they never talked about it. I will miss them, I thought—their friendship, their support, their outlook.

Three days later I got a letter from Basel. And then I started receiving mail from there almost every day. Everything had gone smoothly at the border. Hans wrote that life in Switzerland would not be easy for us, but he was busy making preparations for my arrival. He wrote that he missed me so much, and that he was waiting for me. And with each of his letters I missed him more.

And then it was time for me to go. I put on the gray suit I had worn on my escape from Germany, my best, because it was easier to get through if you were well dressed. Gray flannel suits were very much in fashion then. While still in Berlin, I had told my mother that I wanted to buy one at Wertheim, and she had looked at me in amazement. "You seriously want to buy a suit off the rack in a department store?" Then she pressured me, and to do her a favor more than for any other reason, I went to her tailor and had this elegant piece of clothing made, this suit that I was now wearing with a red scarf on my trip from Prague to Basel. Certainly, no one would have thought that I was an emigrant, especially with the pink lipstick I had bought. It went well with my scarf.

In my compartment, besides me, there was a man in his mid-thirties. He was also well dressed. It so happened that he spoke German quite well. After an exchange of a few sentences, he asked, "Are you from Berlin?"

"Yes," I said. It seemed to be obvious.

"Are you an emigrant?" he asked.

"What makes you think that?"

"You can tell," he said.

"How can you tell?"

"Well, mostly by the way you talk."

The lipstick is not much of a disguise, I thought. And how do I talk?

He was a German emigrant too, on his way to France. He was a writer. Apart from that he didn't say anything about himself; he didn't even mention his name. There was a one-hour layover in Innsbruck, so we went to eat in a small garden café at the station. In the distance the mountains looked beautiful, and it was reassuring to be sitting here with another emigrant instead of eating alone. We didn't have much to say to one another. I thought: Maybe he's worried about his travel documents too. Or maybe he's thinking about someone he's going to see again soon. The way I'm thinking about Hans.

A few hours later we arrived at the border. It went smoothly, without the slightest hitch. I got a simple entry permit stamped into my passport. And then the train rolled into Baden Station in Basel, and there was Hans, without that silly mustache, without the glasses. The way he really was. It was a wonderful reunion.

"Today we're on our honeymoon," he told me. "Our life as emigrants won't begin until tomorrow." He had reserved a room in a hotel; after all, with a fresh entry permit stamped in my passport, for a few days I was here legally, as a tourist.

"The Swabians are here," the receptionist said into the phone.

"Who are the Swabians?" I quietly asked Hans.

"We're the Swabians."

"Why Swabians?"

"Here everyone who comes from Germany is a Swabian, no matter where they're from. And that's the way she's just announced our arrival."

So now we're Swabians. Things are simply different here.

The next day Hans showed me the city, we sat in parks, the way we had done so often in Prague; we had so much to talk about! We walked around for hours. He showed me the Rhine, and it didn't look at all the part, the venerated waterway; it was a yellowish-brown. Along the way, I learned that Greater Basel was on one side of the river and Lesser Basel on the other, and that you could tell the inhabitants apart by the different dialects of Swiss German they spoke.

As illegal refugees we had to live in hiding, never calling attention to ourselves. We were entirely dependent on the help of our Swiss friends. The man who worked in the office, to whom we had been announced as "the Swabians," had offered to help find lodgings for newly arrived emigrants. He sent us to Eddi and Lydia, who had a charming little apartment in Greater Basel.

Eddi was a dining-car waiter, and Hans had made friends with the family. They had a sofa bed in their living room and were prepared to shelter us for a number of months, and then we would move on to live with another Swiss family that was also willing to provide lodging for illegals. That's how things worked here. Sometimes these hosts even provided clothing so that illegals could avoid looking like homeless emigrants and would be less likely to be arrested. Basel was not Prague: in Basel it was very important to be well-dressed like all the good citizens of the city. I was struck by the fact that women wore hats and gloves when they went out in the morning, even if they were only going to the market. Would I ever be able to blend in enough to be inconspicuous here?

Lydia and I got along well. She was one of the few people with whom I didn't feel that she noticed something wrong when she looked at me. "I lived for such a long time in Germany," she said, "that I know how hard it must be for you to adjust to life here. I can tell."

That made me think. "Of course we're different," I said to Hans. "Can they hold that against us?"

He said that we would simply have to try to adjust. "They have their ways, and they judge others according to their own standards . . . sometimes that may seem petty to us, but aren't they also generous in their own way? They are hiding us, giving us shelter, taking care of us. And they're helping us drive fascism out of our country. Isn't that generous? And courageous?"

"Still, things are often difficult, especially for emigré women," I said.

"Swiss women look at me and say, 'The poor thing can't even knit.' 'The poor thing,' that's me. It's true, I can't knit, I never wanted to learn, but I had no idea this could be held against me. It's different for you, no one cares whether you knit or not. You don't have to be like all the other men here. When you smoke, that's just the way you are. If I smoke, it's a scandal."

Here it's impossible to have committees for illegals. But there were Swiss families who made sure that we had enough to eat. Every weekday we ate dinner with a different family; this we did out of caution, as well as a desire not to overburden any one family.

Everything was so different! Hans had even changed his name: he was now called Stephan. It would be too dangerous to be known by his real name here; for the time being Hans Fittko would have to disappear. There was that case of the Spandau storm trooper who had been murdered by his own buddies: that was pinned on Hans Fittko, after the "takeover." And the Czech banishment for life, which the Gestapo had to know about. We were sitting here dangerously close to the border.

But what an advantage that was!

A large share of the antifascist literature was produced here in Basel. Members of the printers' unions helped us here too. Flyers, calls to continue the struggle, and brochures were all regularly published: Against War and Fascism! End the Terror! Down with the Hitler Dictatorship! We even began to disguise some of our material by binding it into innocent-looking covers. We used all kinds of titles, titles for owners' manuals, advertisements for cosmetics, cookbooks, a Reclam Edition of *Hermann und Dorothea*. It was easier, and a little less dangerous, to get these across the border and put them into distribution.

Over there we had set up enough drop-off points to cover the entire state of Baden. Swiss and German antifascists, on both sides of the border, helped to expand our network. There were Communists, Social Democrats, union members, and newcomers who found their way to us. Just as political prisoners in concentration camps had done, we would overcome the divisions that had previously existed among the various antifascist groups.

Basel, where the borders of three countries intersect, was a natural center for illegal traffic. But without the help of our Swiss friends we would never have been able to set up our network. There were a lot of people from Basel who had jobs across the border in Germany, most in the vicinity of Lörrach, just as there were many Germans who worked in

Basel, most of them at Ciba Pharmaceuticals. Mornings and evenings there was very heavy border traffic—bicycles, pedestrians, streetcar commuters; you could easily lose yourself in the crowd. The only identification you needed was a border pass, and it was easy to get if you had friends among the Swiss who worked in Germany. Taking adequate precautions, you could even smuggle people from other regions across the border. Precautions: that meant, for example, keep quiet so as not to be recognized as a "Swabian." Dress like the inhabitants of the region. Simply put, do not call attention to yourself. Smuggle the literature across in ways that the Gestapo did not yet suspect: inside bicycle frames, in jacket linings, in the false bottoms of shopping bags, under truck seats.

From time to time we used other methods, often with the help of personal contacts. On Wednesdays, Stephan ate with Family G. After dinner, Stephan and Herr G. often played chess and talked, enjoying each other's company. Herr G. was not a political person, but he was adamant in his opposition to national socialism. Herr G. was a customs inspector. Through him, with the help of stamps and permits, we were occasionally able to get large packets, and sometimes even crates, across the border into Germany.

Many young German Jews, no longer permitted to study inside the Reich, continued their educations at the University of Basel. Their parents stayed on in Germany; the students had valid travel documents and could reside in Switzerland legally. We made friends with a group of these students. They often visited their parents and took messages back and forth across the border.

One of the women students in this group set up a drop-off point for us at the Baden railroad station. At first Ruth carefully surveyed the situation and then reported to us. She made a drawing of what appeared to be the best site. It was some distance—but not too far —from the barrier separating the German zone from the Swiss part of the station, in case an emergency crossing became necessary. An iron fence separated the German and the Swiss areas, all the way from the barrier to the other end of the hall.

A man was approaching this fence. I didn't know him. I don't even know today who he was. He was simply one of us. Judging by the train schedule, he had just arrived from Freiburg. Average height, brown hair, gray felt hat, gray coat, black shoes. About thirty years old. The way you might imagine someone to look who had *"Special Characteristics: None"* noted in his passport. He was carrying a brown briefcase, similar to mine.

Everything was as Ruth had described it. Yes, but wasn't this method somehow very foolish? Without knowing each other? Or maybe it was better not to know each other? The man was approaching the fence . . . heading for a particular spot. Our eyes had met, briefly, and he had shot a quick glance at my briefcase. There was no question; we had "recognized" one another.

The man set his briefcase down near the fence. At this point the bars did not entirely reach to the floor. For a moment I had been unnerved, but now I was calm again. We greeted each other like old friends who had met just by chance. I put my briefcase down and we talked for a while, very casually. No one was watching us. With my foot, I began slowly pushing my briefcase in his direction, under the bars. It fit through the open space. He did the same with his case. For a moment I thought: My God, I'm standing here with one foot on German territory! I kept pushing the case, very slowly . . . and now it was in Germany. It had all gone very smoothly!

We were in agreement with our contacts across the border: the literature we produced here in Switzerland would have a greater impact if, besides slogans and calls to take up the struggle against national socialism, we also reported on current events, on what was happening in factories where we had contacts, for example. We needed to report on things like increased exploitation, Gestapo spies, the Terror and arrests, war preparations in the arms industry.

We received many reports from the Karlsruhe munitions plant about conditions there; we had several contacts. Of them, Rudolf was the single most important source of information, and his reports came regularly. And because he was allowed entry into several different departments, we could make good use of his information in our publications without drawing undue attention to him. He had relatives in Basel and often came to visit, and we were able to sit down and discuss our work with him.

On one of his visits he asked to talk with us in a safe place, and we went to Lydia's apartment.

"I want to show you something," he said. He had blueprints with him and spread them out on the kitchen table.

He pointed with his finger: "Do you know what this is?"

Stephan, and two of his friends who had come with us, studied the drawings.

"Dumdum bullets!"

"Fantastic, Rudolf!"

"But you have to be careful with things like this," said Stephan. "If they catch you with it, things could get more than a little unpleasant for you."

"I know. Don't worry. I was thinking what an impact this could have if we got it published."

"Of course. We have to think this through carefully. Maybe one of the pacifist publicists could make good use of it. I'm thinking of someone like Berthold Jacob, for example."

Our involvement with another event was purely coincidental: Edmund's arrest.

For the most part, when German emigrants were arrested, they were arrested out on the streets, but sometimes the police also searched bars, garden cafés, and even streetcars—wherever the emigrants were conspicuous because of their accents, their looks, or often their worn clothing. Sometimes it was simply their behavior that marked them as "Swabians."

An arrested emigrant was taken to the Police Presidium and locked up for not having a valid residence permit. Among the emigrants the jail at Lohenhof was known as the highest mountain in Switzerland, because it took ten days to descend from the "summit." And then the emigrant was unceremoniously "shoved across" the border out of Switzerland. At this time, to their credit, the Swiss were dumping emigrants into St. Louis rather than Lörrach, into France instead of Germany. The poor, resourceless, often unshaven emigrants would be quickly spotted by the French police and taken to the *gendarmerie*. At least they would have a roof over their heads for the night, but they often suffered miserable treatment at the hands of the police: being pushed around, cursed, and jailed for days, without any contact with the outside.

After about a week in jail, they would be taken back to the Swiss border. At that time the French did not force their prisoners back across the border into Germany. But, depending on their mood, they would sometimes set the emigrants free or, more often, take them directly to a Swiss border crossing, where the Swiss police immediately took them into custody and hauled them back to the Presidium. It went back and forth like this until the emigrants somehow managed to disappear: at the border crossing, in St. Louis, or in Basel. Sometimes Swiss friends were able to help. Peppi, our friend from the French-speaking part of the country, was especially inventive in these matters. When he heard that someone in St. Louis was in danger of being "returned," he would go to the border to see what he could do.

Once, it was a young emigrant named Erich who was about to be given the shove. At the very moment the Swiss police were to take him into custody, he ran. Peppi was standing on a corner watching what was happening. Erich ran toward an approaching streetcar, the two border police on his heels. Peppi shouted, "Come back, come back, hurry!" and waved his arms wildly in the air. The police stopped and turned around: "What's wrong? What's happening?" Erich jumped onto the streetcar and it left, with Erich, and Peppi yelled to the police: "I didn't mean you. I meant him, that one over there."

Edmund had been arrested on the street. The usual routine. Jailed by the police, shoved across the border into St. Louis, French jail, then back to Basel. We met in a tavern. "I have something to tell you," he said. "Monsieur le Commissaire of St. Louis has invited me to dinner."

"Go on!"

On the second night of Edmund's stay in jail, the superintendent had come to his cell. He was friendly and asked Edmund if he was being well treated. Edmund saw this as an opportunity to complain and said, first of all, that they were being fed some awful slop. He was very sorry, said the superintendent, and he would be happy to offer Edmund a pleasant meal, with a little wine, if Edmund would accept his invitation to dinner. Now Edmund was really curious.

"And then? What happened then?" Stephan asked.

"He asked me to pass along a dinner invitation to you. He'd also like to have dinner with you. Including a little wine, I assume."

"Dinner with me . . . what's that supposed to mean? Who am I?"

"You are Stephan. He's heard about you, and he's very interested in meeting you, he said. And then he added: We—you and he—have mutual interests. He wanted me to tell you that you would not regret it, and neither would I. One hand washes the other, he said. Then I wanted to know where he had heard your name, and why he wanted to meet you especially. When you work so close to the border, you get curious, he said. According to what he had heard, you are well-informed, and he thought that the two of you might exchange information. That was all I could get out of him."

"And it's all pretty clear," said Stephan. "But the fact that he knows my name, that's very peculiar. Something's leaking somewhere."

"Do you intend to meet him?"

"No. Too fishy. We want to help our comrades with their struggle at home. Spying may sometimes be appropriate, but we have to keep our focus! Just think how dangerous that could be for our contacts back home."

"I understand," said Edmund. "But me, I've gotten into this mess the same way the Virgin got her child, and now I'm curious. How does all this fit together? What does the guy know? I think I should go back again and talk to him."

Stephan thought for a while. "If you want to play the messenger, maybe it's a good opportunity for us."

"I could do it," said Edmund. "He gave me a border pass and promised me regal treatment if I bring him an answer." He thought. "And what answer shall I give him?"

"The reply is that Stephan will not even consider meeting an official who treats our emigrants so poorly. Monsieur le Commissaire would first have to make sure that, from now on, people who are forced across the border into France are treated like refugees, with a right to asylum. The funny business has to stop. The emigrants can't simply be shoved back across the border into Switzerland. So, that's my answer."

"And then?" Edmund asked.

"Then? We'll see. Tell him that Stephan hasn't made a final decision."

The following week, the first emigrant to be forced over the border into France had nothing but good things to say about his treatment. The French had released him some distance from the Swiss border, and he should feel free to report this to his friends in Switzerland, they said.

"You have done us all a great service," Stephan told Edmund. "More and more German Jews now want to leave the country."

"But how long are we going to be able to keep the superintendent happy?" asked Edmund.

"We keep our options open as long as possible, and we make no commitments."

"Stephan, I'm not sure—but don't you think we should work a little more closely with the man? Isn't anything done in opposition to the Nazi regime a part of our cause, too?"

"Not necessarily. Not when we can't trust our partner's intentions."

# TRI-COUNTRY BORDER

If you had legal documents you could simply get on a streetcar in Basel and go to France, and the French could likewise take a streetcar into Switzerland or Germany. Of course, there was also automobile traffic. It only took about fifteen minutes to reach Basel from Germany or to go from Basel into the Third Reich—we referred to it as "over there" or "home," because we knew that this insanity could not last and that we would soon be going home.

But, for as long as it did last, this proximity of three countries had created a set of unusual opportunities. Secret plans for German weapons production fell into our hands. France's Intelligence Service was ready, through Le Commissaire, to do us favors in return for information to which only we had access. We were able to put pressure on the French secret police, who wanted the cooperation of an emigrant named Stephan.

It was Stephan's idea to contact the journalist Berthold Jacob to show him the blueprints. He was the right man; for years he had specialized in uncovering illegal preparations for war.

But things did not work out as planned.

We had no idea that Berthold Jacob was in Basel. Apparently he wanted to follow up on some signal he had received. He met his contacts in a restaurant in the city, and they were to take him to the people who had the information he wanted. A car was ready to take him to the appointed meeting.

The next morning, in the newspaper, we read about what had happened.

"That idiot!" Stephan cursed, and you could see the blood rising to his head. "That fool! Didn't anything strike him as being suspicious? Wasn't he supposed to be experienced? Was he blind? Just got into the car!"

The car in which Berthold Jacob was riding had sped straight across the border into Germany. He was in the hands of the Gestapo.

Were there any cross-contacts? Maybe the French secret police knew something more about the case. Jacob was generally known to be a Francophile. How had he been lured into this trap? Was there any connection with the information we had been given? With our people over there? We didn't have any answers, but we all knew that anyone who had any possible connection with this case would have to be more alert than ever. There was something very strange going on here.

In the meantime we had moved into Widow Gittli's apartment; she had an extra room for us. Here the two of us could finally be alone as much as we wanted—and here I could finally call my husband Hans again. Still, Widow Gittli was always grumbling because I never washed the dishes quite the way she wanted, even though I tried very hard. I could never remember whether I was supposed to rinse the dishes in hot water or cold. No matter how I did it, it always seemed to be wrong.

When she was angry, she made a face like a bulldog. Once, when I started to boil potatoes, she made a great fuss and said she was surprised to see me cooking something so complicated. She made me very nervous, and all the while I had to take great care to be nice to her. After all, it was very generous of her to give us shelter, and we needed her. Stephan, on the other hand, never gave her any cause for criticism.

"Why are you so jumpy?" Hans asked. "Is it because of Jacob?" I had already dropped the milk jug for a second time that day.

"Actually, it's because of Widow Gittli," I said.

Hans laughed. "You seem to be more afraid of her than you are of the secret police of three different countries!"

"And it's Thursday, too, the day I eat at Karl's."

"But you like Karl, don't you?"

"Yes, I like him, and he means well—too well. I get unnerved just thinking about it."

Karl ran a little restaurant in the city. He was big and strong, wore a white hat on his head and a striped apron over his large belly. He served his guests spaghetti and beer in a small garden. When I went there on Thursdays, he always said he would fatten me up; it just wouldn't do to have a skinny little thing like me in Switzerland. Naturally I was hungry, but when he appeared with his giant pot and ladled spaghetti into my huge bowl, I lost my appetite because I knew that I would never, in all my life, be able to eat it all. And if I left anything in my bowl Karl would be insulted and would say that his spaghetti wasn't good enough for me, and I was afraid we would lose a place to eat. Why shouldn't I be nervous?

"Thank you, Karl, thank you," I say and swallow hard, before I've eaten my first bite. "Your spaghetti is delicious, the best I have ever eaten, but I can't eat so much, my stomach isn't big enough. . . ."

"That isn't even enough to keep a tiny bird alive," Karl claimed. "Here, another little spoonful . . ." Just so long as I don't get sick! If I eat very slowly, maybe I can do it. But no, here he comes again, out of the kitchen with his ladle . . .

He is so kind, Karl is.

Our delivery network was expanded. The Gestapo hadn't managed to track down any of our carriers and no one had been arrested.

Hermann drove a truck for his company. Most of the time he hauled a cargo of building materials. The truck was loaded in Switzerland and goods were delivered to various points in Germany. About twice a month Hermann notified our friends in Basel that his route would allow him to make deliveries to our drop-off sites.

The packets of literature were loaded onto the truck in his garage. Our helpers were practiced and worked quickly. It was a very safe method of transport, and a lot of material was delivered this way. Robert, the second driver, had been clued in. He also knew where the packets were hidden.

As always, the loading was finished by evening, and after a couple of hours of sleep, Hermann and Robert left in the dark.

It wasn't clear what caught their attention, maybe it was a sound. At any rate, they stopped along the still empty highway. Robert jumped out and checked. Then he signaled Hermann to get out too.

As far as they could see, the highway behind them was strewn with a ribbon of packets. Some had broken open from the fall, releasing flyers into the air and scattering them across the surface of the road. Time to get out of here, get out of here fast, onto a side road that led into the forest along the highway.

Packets continued to fall. Deep in the forest they stopped and crawled under the truck. Luckily, they each had a knife. They could see what had happened: the strap they had used to tie the packets under the chassis was torn. After they had cut all the packets free from the truck, they drove on to Germany with their legal cargo.

They later heard a report that the Gestapo had found a few bundles of flyers and brochures in the woods near the highway. The perpetrators were never found.

Lydia often talked about Basel's famous Carnival, and she wanted us to see it all. It did not surprise me that Stephan showed very little interest, I had never known him to have any enthusiasm for the kind of festivities being described to us. But I was curious, and Lydia spent weeks making preparations. She went as a gypsy, despite her blond hair and blue eyes. She dressed me up as a milkmaid, and I couldn't even yodel. I felt a little silly, but I was sure no one would recognize us behind our masks.

We went to the parade together. Lydia's husband, Eddi, came with us. And somehow he was even able to persuade Stephan to come along. We were astounded! I thought I knew the good citizens of Basel, they are proper and well-mannered. But apparently not when they're wearing masks.

There was an endless procession of costumed people, as well as papier-mâché figures of politicians, mendicant musicians, artists, and dancers. The finest examples of many arts. Where were these talents hidden throughout the rest of the year? Who made these wonderfully clever placards? Who were all these people dancing around full of good cheer and high spirits?

Was this my friend Lydia, the good little housewife, who was dragging me into overcrowded bars? I knew her mask, but otherwise I would not have believed what this shameless wench was up to. The giggling gypsy tease, surrounded by throngs of men taking improper liberties, as they say ... I had never seen anything like it, not even on New Year's Eve on the Kurfürstendamm, not even on the Place Pigalle. Or had I become so prim and proper myself? I looked around for Hans, but both husbands had disappeared. The gypsy, Lydia, grabbed me, the milkmaid, by the arm and headed off into one bar after the other. Nothing, to put it mildly, was in particularly good taste, but it was something new, and I had to see what was going on in this world. Along the way we met other emigrants we knew, and they were behaving just as wildly as the Baselers. This went on for days, until weaving and exhausted figures finally dragged themselves home.

I had already noticed during the first stage of our emigration, in Prague, that some of us now felt attracted to diversions we had previously scorned. Serious people I had gotten to know through discussions, people who might be inclined to seek entertainment in a chess game—here of all places, and now of all times—had begun to spend their nights in dance clubs, the kind you find a few steps down from street level. There they sat with a glass of beer, trying to get a dance with a Czech girl, and trying to make themselves understood. It was true that they had nothing better to do in Prague. But it seemed that many of the emigrants had become addicted to the search for pleasure. I wondered if great calamities always affect people this way, and it made me think of the plague.

Birthdays were celebrated wherever there was space for a few people, and whenever there was enough money to buy a few bottles of Pils. Whenever there was something to celebrate, people drank and carried on with abandon. I thought about New Year's Eve in Berlin, where we got together and were happy; but we hadn't felt anything like this feverish hunger for distraction.

In Basel, everyone had to be much more careful, but there were still many occasions to celebrate. I remember one evening at Lydia's when we were drinking lots of different Alsatian wines. Too much wine for me, as it turned out, because Stephan had a hard time getting me home. This had never happened to me before. What were we celebrating? It doesn't matter. We *had* to be able to take our minds off things!

Stephan kept checking the time. "What time are you expecting George?" I asked.

"Sepp went across on his motorcycle to pick him up. They must already be in Lörrach."

"You seem to be certain that he'll come." I said. "Yet he must be worried about what's going to happen here."

"But there's no other way out for him."

No way out. That's how it is. A weak moment and they've got you in their grasp, because there's no way back either. You no longer have any comrades because you've become a traitor.

"He set up contacts and carried literature over the border," Stephan said, as he paced back and forth in the small room. "He doesn't lack courage. Can he be judged for lacking strength?" He stopped in front of the window and looked over at me.

"That's not the issue now!"

"I know, what we have to do now is make sure he does no more harm. We have to know what he told them, we have to make sure—no matter

what the cost!—that no one else gets arrested. Through him they can roll
up every group in Baden."

"Do we know it was him?" I asked. "Are you sure, and are you sure
he'll come?"

"He has to come, otherwise he'll only confirm our suspicions, and
then he knows he'll be done for. On both sides—here and over there."

Yes, he has to. Sometimes the strong ones become weak, and the weak
ones remain strong. You ask yourself, why this and not that one, and you
can't find an answer. But whoever it may be, whoever fails to hold out, we
cannot tolerate it, because that would mean the end of the resistance. You
learn to depend on nothing and no one.

Stephan looked up at the clock again. "We'll meet at Lydia's, the
usual location. Lydia knows what this is about."

"Well, what's happening, what's all the rush?" George asked as he walked
into the room, smiling. He was so self-assured that you could almost
imagine we were mistaken.

"Sit down," Stephan said, pointing to the chair across the table. Sepp
and Willi were already seated at the round table in Lydia's dining room.
The sun shone through the curtains, sending a delicate pattern of shadows into their midst.

"We brought you out because we want to talk to you. And yes, we're
in a hurry. Something's gone wrong over there, as you know, but you
haven't told us anything about it. However it may have happened, it's happened, and now you have to help us save . . . "

"What are you talking about?" George interrupted, looking into
Stephan's face, astounded. His voice was steady. He sat there, lean and
bony, with the same straight posture he always had those many times they
had sat around this table and discussed the work to be done over there.
But his hands. He could no longer control his hands, he tugged distract-
edly at his jacket sleeve with his fingers. The truth. We had to get the
truth out of him!

"We are talking about the fact," Stephan said slowly, "that you were
arrested, and that following your arrest your contacts were nabbed."

George jumped up.

"Wait," said Stephan, signaling with his hand for George to sit down.
He took a piece of paper out of his pocket and looked at it. "First, on
Monday, two weeks ago, you pick up material here, as always. Two days
later the handbills show up in your factory. That afternoon you disappear;

not even your wife knows where you are, and you are gone for four days. Let me finish." He looked at the piece of paper again. "The following Monday, you return home, but you don't leave the house, not even to go to work. Someone sees you at the window, and pretty soon everyone knows about how you look, about how they worked you over."

"You're imagining things," said George. His fingers gripped the edge of the table. "I had to go to the dentist, my cheek was swollen. It was an infection, I had a fever and had to stay home." He looked around the room and continued to speak, his agitation growing: "Anyway, what do you want from me? How dare you . . . ? You've got the wrong man!"

Stephan looked at him. "On Tuesday, Fritz is arrested; the next day, Käthe. And for four days the Gestapo has been sitting at our drop-off site, waiting for more of our people to show up."

"Don't delude yourself, George," Sepp said. "It is obvious that you're the only one they could have gotten it from, but I wanted proof in any case. Before I picked you up, I talked to a few of our friends over there. They showed me a note."

"Are you trying to force a confession out of me? And you really think I'll fall for all these old police tricks!"

"How did that meeting with Otto go?" Sepp asked. "He would have been caught if he hadn't noticed you were being tailed."

"It was me who saved him!" George shouted. "I didn't go up to him, I looked away and gave him time to escape. Do you know what they would have done if they . . ." He suddenly interrupted himself, and then, with fright and anger in his voice, he said, ". . . and now you think you've got me in your trap—."

Stephan raised his hand. "No one believes you wanted to get Otto arrested. But in a weak moment you gave in and told them about the meeting. Or you wrote it down on a piece of paper and they found the note. Now you have to tell us the truth, George. Everything! What else did they get out of you? Which names? What do they know about border crossings? Are other contacts in danger?"

Silence.

"The biggest mistake you could make is not to tell us everything. It would not be in your best interests to withhold information."

"You have no right to threaten me!" George yelled, in a shrill voice. "What are you planning to do with me?" His eyes raced around the room from one of us to the other.

Willi stood up and walked with his heavy gait around the table.

George twitched slightly and stared after him.

"What are you planning to do with me?" he yelled again. He reached for the arms of his chair and started to get up, his hands shaking. Willi looked at George, then turned his back on him and walked into the kitchen. In the stillness you could hear dishes clinking. George fell back into his chair, but his eyes kept moving. We heard Willi's footsteps coming back into the room, and George shot a glance toward the door. Willi stood there, his massive figure filling the doorway. He was holding a cup in his hand, slurping down coffee.

"George, we have not brought you here to take revenge on you," said Stephan. "We have to make sure there are no more arrests, and you are going to help us. You know those thugs over there aren't finished with you. They are going to force you to betray more and more of what you know."

"I am not a traitor! What do *you* know, anyway? Here you sit, high and dry on the outside, you haven't got a clue what we poor slobs have to face; what do you mean by strong? no one can take it . . ." He swallowed a sob.

The room was quiet. The hum of bees drifted in to us through the half-open window.

"You said you are no traitor," Stephan finally broke the silence. "I know it isn't the role you sought for yourself. But you gave them the names of your comrades, and we have to see what we can still save. The Gestapo's never going to let you go. And once you've gotten all our friends yanked, they'll have you make new contacts, they'll make a provocateur out of you. They'll drag you deeper and deeper into the swamp, and when there's nothing more to get out of you, well, you know. . . . "

"You—all of you, you're worse than the Gestapo!" George shouted. He wiped the perspiration from his forehead with the back of his hand.

"There is only one way out," Stephan continued. "You tell us everything that happened over there and you stay here on the outside. You'll be safe here, we can see to it."

"Stay here on the outside? You're crazy! How can I stay here? Just leave home, just disappear, and never go back?"

"Think about what's waiting for you over there."

George's face was yellow. "Yes, I'm thinking. Just let me go back home once more. When I've taken care of the most important things, I'll come back. I can't just leave my wife and child without seeing them, you have to understand!"

"We do understand," said Willi, from the doorway, "and we gave it some thought. If you go back, you'll be at their mercy again. But I can bring your wife out and you can discuss things here. If she wants to follow you with the child, we can shelter you here for a time; our Swiss friends will help."

George sat there, his shoulders drooping, exhausted, his red eyes staring into empty space. "I'll stay here, a leper," he said with a heavy tongue.

"You're worse than the Gestapo!" he had shouted. No, we are not the Gestapo, we do not use their methods. But we had to put pressure on him, there was nothing else for us to do.

What we have to do here is not easy.

# BETRAYAL

$P$eter was one of the youngest among us. He came from the Ruhr region, had fled first to Luxembourg, and then finally landed here. We liked being with him. Berti, his young girlfriend from Basel, was with him much of the time. Both of them were always cheerful, and their good humor even helped to keep our spirits up.

Peter was providing lodging for George and his family. I wasn't sure where, but I assumed that it must be somewhere in France. You could count on Peter; he never lost his nerve.

We were sitting together over a glass of wine in our favorite pub. We had made friends with Franz, the hefty owner, and felt quite safe here in his care. We talked about how we could reestablish contacts that had been broken off over there when George was arrested. How could we do it without endangering others? Who of our friends was still there? How would we find new coworkers? Was there anyone who knew people over there, and had experience—someone who could help rebuild our groups?

"I'll go across," said Peter, "I know the area. And I know a few people too. Maybe I can get some old and new crossings and establish some drop-off sites."

Stephan looked at him for a long time. "Think it over carefully," he said. "We can talk about it."

About a week later, Peter went across. He melded into the early-morning crowds going from Switzerland to work in the factories around Lörrach. He wore work clothes and, as we had discussed, carried no luggage, only a bag with his lunch. He had learned all of the names and addresses by heart; he had written nothing down, not one single note. He was very responsible and understood how to carry out a project like this.

It was several weeks before we heard from him again. That was to be expected. Peter had to have time to settle in. Then, suddenly, there was a short message from Freiburg: the entire group there had been arrested. Nothing about Peter.

It was a bad sign that we still hadn't heard anything from him. Where could he be?

A few days passed. Then Gerhard, our courier from Heilbronn, arrived. Our friends in Heilbronn had been arrested shortly after the group in Freiburg. He, Gerhard, had managed to get away. Peter had barely set foot in Heilbronn before being arrested along with everyone else. Was he in the hands of the Gestapo? Would there be a trial? No one knew anything.

First of all, we had to warn everyone who might now be in danger because of the arrests. And of course we had to tell Berti everything that had happened. I had heard that she had become more and more unsettled over this past week. How easily I could empathize with her!

Stephan sent a friend to tell me: Go see Berti immediately. Her family can't cope.

When I saw her I was shocked. She was sobbing, her arms flailing in the air, she was screaming. I knew I would not be able to calm her down. There isn't much anyone can say when a thing like this happens, and she wasn't listening to me at all. Her abdomen was swollen, she was groaning with pain. As quickly as we could, we found a doctor we could trust. He came and gave her a shot that quieted her somewhat. She was in pain, he explained, because in her agitated state she was swallowing too much air. I sat by her bed all night, a night I will never forget.

Peter was sentenced to five years in prison. The others received sentences of between five to ten years. None of those arrested made any statement.

Peter had intended to enlist with the International Brigades in Spain. Stephan had thought about this as well, but after everything that had happened here, it was very difficult to make that kind of decision. Where was he needed more?

Emigrants from various countries who wanted to go to Spain had to be brought across the border here. As did people in Germany, who had been exposed there and wanted to continue the fight in Spain. Now, of all times, when our crossings had just been blown away! We had to rebuild them. And we still had to keep Le Commissaire of St. Louis in a good mood. We badly needed his help with all of this work. We would have to throw him a harmless scrap of information now and then. He was still insisting on a meeting with the man named Stephan.

I had thought through this situation again and again. I had also been asking myself: which is more dangerous? Not that it depended on me, but where would I worry less about Stephan? On the German border or on the Spanish front? There was really no difference between the two.

In the end, he realized how desperately he was needed here.

Now our main task was to establish new contacts. There had been an increase in the number of people who wanted to help with the border work, and some of them were experienced. We were talking to Ewald, a man from Spandau.

Since I had gotten to know Hans, we always seemed to be coming across people from Spandau. During all the years I had lived in Berlin, Spandau had been a part of the city I seldom seemed to visit, and I knew very few people there. For Hans and his friends Spandau was home. It almost seemed as if they looked upon Berlin as a suburb of Spandau. And it really was so: whichever direction we were thrown in our emigration, we always seemed to find a circle of old acquaintances, friends, and helpers—among them always someone from Spandau. Some of them had known each other since their days in elementary school, and most of them knew each other's families, too. They had been drawn together by their shared struggle against a growing fascist threat. Almost all of them knew Hans Fittko; and he had been only eighteen years old when he was elected chairman of the Spandau Unemployment Council.

Of course, Ewald the Spandauer wanted to help. As did a number of others.

I was home alone. At the time, we were living with a married couple in the city, just beyond Baden Station. Here, we had our own room in a small house, and it was lovely. They were extraordinarily kind and friendly toward us, but unfortunately often fought with one another. The husband was from Tessin and accordingly temperamental. His mixture of Italian and Swiss-German was difficult to understand. Even his wife had trouble; so there was a lot of screaming in the house.

It was early one morning and I had just gotten up. Stephan had gone to Zurich for three days to meet with a few friends from over there. The first thing I heard was the doorbell, then a short conversation, followed by a knock on our door. A young man I didn't know stood there and said he had to speak to me.

"District Attorney Gans sent me," he said. "He asks that you come to his office immediately."

The district attorney? This could hardly be anything good. I had

once met Dr. Gans briefly; Stephan knew him better. All I knew was that
he was a Social Democrat, that he was a Jew, and that he was not nega-
tively disposed toward us.

"Please sit down," Dr. Gans greeted me. "I have something to discuss
with you, and it must go no further."

He wanted to know where my husband was. In Zurich, I explained; I
was expecting him back the next evening. What did we need to discuss?
Was there anything I could do in the meantime?

Yes, said Dr. Gans, and the matter was most urgent. I had to make
sure that my husband did not return from Zurich to Basel.

"What do you mean, Herr Doktor?"

"The German Reich has filed an extradition request for your husband
with the Swiss federal government."

"Extradition! On what basis? For murder? Rape? Robbery? That's
what they do now when they want to get their hands on their political
opponents!"

"Yes, precisely—murder. Unfortunately it's no joke. The warrant
actually claims that your husband is wanted for a recently committed
murder. Here are the files. Of course, I am counting on your discretion
and expecting that this matter will go no further."

At this point I grew hot with fear.

"Read it for yourself," said Dr. Gans. "Here is the extradition request:
'. . . for murder . . .' But that's not all. Keep reading: The Swiss Federal
Government will honor this request."

Was that really possible?

Yes, I guess that really could be possible!

"And then, here: the subject is known by the name of Stephan. Family name unknown."

Thank god! They didn't know who Stephan was.

"Do you know what this document is? 'The Man Known as Stephan,'
yes, it is a warrant: 'Address unknown, residence in the area behind Baden
Station, . . . alternates wearing a gray suit and a dark blue suit.' Then:
approximate age, height, weight. Additional: gap in front teeth, left side,
causing a slight lisp. And so on. Read this page and you will understand
why I had to speak with you immediately. The federal government has
agreed not only to honor the request but actively to search for the man
known as Stephan. Swiss special forces are now on their way to Basel for
this express purpose."

It was known that there was close cooperation between certain high-ranking Swiss police officials and the Gestapo. . . .

"I hope you can keep your husband from returning to Basel. I certainly don't have to explain how dangerous his situation is—especially here in Basel, but he's in danger everywhere in Switzerland."

Naturally. But what was I to do now? How could I reach him in time in Zurich? All I had was the address of his friends where he was staying. I didn't even know them. First I had to find someone willing to go to Zurich to warn Stephan. None of the emigrants, that would be too dangerous. It had to be a Swiss. Whom could I turn to?

It wasn't easy. I talked to a few of our friends, but the men worked during the day, and the women couldn't just up and leave the house and their children behind. There was not even a late train to Zurich.

Then I remembered Peppi and went to talk to his wife, Marie. She was able to get hold of him at work. Okay, he said, I'll take my motorbike to Zurich. He would come back that same night; I should wait for him with Marie in order to find out if he'd been successful.

Later, in Marie's kitchen, I thought: How did the Gestapo get its information about Stephan? Who could have provided such an exact description, including the most minute details, like the gap between his front teeth?

Suddenly, it occurred to me: When Dr. Gans showed me the warrant in his office, I had seen a note. "Source of the following information is Fräulein Hilde K." The last name had been crossed out.

Could that be—? Yes, I knew who that was.

Ludwig, one of our friends from over there, was engaged to a girl in Basel, and her name was Hilde. Ludwig came from the area around Lörrach. He had been one of our contacts for a long time. A few weeks before, he had been arrested and tortured, but he had not made a statement. We were told that Hilde had visited him in jail. I also knew that Hilde lived in the same part of Basel we did. We had met her through Ludwig, and one evening some time before Ludwig's arrest, Stephan and I had met her and stopped to talk for a while.

That was it: the Gestapo had promised to release Ludwig if Hilde would provide information about Ludwig's contacts in Basel. These were well-known Gestapo tactics.

Once, in a conversation, I remembered Ludwig saying, Hilde isn't interested in politics, she doesn't understand anything about it. When he was arrested she was desperate and couldn't bear the thought of his being tortured. She did what was demanded of her in order to get him released.

Did she really understand what she had done? Certainly. Did she have a bad conscience? Hardly. This was her Ludwig, after all. What she did was terrible. But it wasn't surprising.

Peppi had not been able to find Stephan in Zurich. But he had spoken with the people at whose apartment Stephan was staying and gave them a short urgent letter for him.

It was late and I went home. "Be very careful," said Marie. "The special forces may have already surrounded that section of the city."

The streets were empty and dark. I didn't notice anything out of the ordinary.

As I climbed the steps to our room, I noticed how tired I was. It had been a long, strenuous day, a distressing day. But we had avoided the worst. Hans would certainly get in contact with me in the morning.

In the room I turned on the light. Hans was lying in bed. "Where do you spend your nights while I'm out of town?" he asked. This was one of his jokes, but I knew him—he had apparently been quite upset when he found an empty bed on his return.

That's all we needed. The man known as Stephan to be upset. I had to sit down.

"Why did you come back today? Did you notice anything on your way home?"

"Notice what? I finished early. What are you talking about?"

"How did you get back? They've probably surrounded this whole area in order to catch you! You have to get away from here, they're out to get you . . ." I told him everything. "What should we do?"

Hans had gotten out of bed and was pacing around the room. "At this moment, nothing—until morning. I need three, at the most four, days to make sure our network doesn't fall apart."

I wanted to say, "You aren't thinking of offering yourself up on a serving platter, are you?" But it wouldn't have made any difference, I couldn't have stopped him from following through with his plans. I knew that he was going to take care to transfer his network, just as he had done when he was banned from Czechoslovakia.

The next morning I went into the city alone and then sent word that he could come out, I hadn't seen any police. Until our departure, Hans stayed with Lydia and Eddi; I stayed with Marie and Peppi. Friends went to our apartment to pick up the things we needed most. Hans asked the people who were going to take over our contacts to meet him at Lydia's. He didn't leave the apartment once during those four days—four days that were difficult for me to bear, and certainly for him too. But he didn't show it, he seemed very calm, as if he were completing some normal business transaction. I knew how things would go: once everything had been completed and had gone smoothly, then his nerves would show. Then he would start talking in his sleep and I would have to shake him until he woke up. He said he had started talking in his sleep during the last year he spent in Berlin: in his sleep he was making speeches at Nazi rallies, and his sisters had hardly been able to wake him.

By the fourth day the work was done. Our friends made preparations for an "excursion to the country." A small group of men went through the fields with Hans. They were familiar with the area; they knew exactly where they would be safe, where they were in no danger of falling into the hands of customs officers or border patrols. On the French side of the border they went directly to a bar and drank a glass of Alsatian wine. They clinked glasses. Peppi went with Hans to the train station and bought him a ticket to Mulhouse.

In the meantime, along with a group of Swiss friends, I took the streetcar to St. Louis. We carried the usual shopping bags, and some of my friends had even brought along yarn and needles and began knitting. I still hadn't learned to knit properly, despite my two-and-one-half-year stay in Switzerland. We were a cheerful bunch, we babbled on and laughed a lot. I laughed too, but I didn't talk much because my Swiss-German had an unmistakable Swabian ring. At the checkpoint we showed our passes, as did all of the passengers. I had a pass too.

We didn't want to stop in St. Louis for long. After brief good-byes we parted, and Marie went with me to the train station. I bought a ticket and waited for the next train to Mulhouse. There I would meet Stephan; no, Hans.

# HOLLAND

In Amsterdam it seemed to me that only a few days had passed since we had met in Mulhouse. I stood in front of the fireplace and turned every few minutes or so to warm myself in the heat of the flames, from the front, from the back, and then from the sides. Unless you were standing directly in front of the fireplace, the large room was cold and damp, like the air in Amsterdam.

In Mulhouse I had gone up to the ticket window and asked for two tickets to Paris, just like that; we were, after all, in France. Marie had very carefully instructed me how to say, without an accent: *"Deux billets pour Paris . . ."*—no, the *p* was not followed by an *h*. . . .

Then we were sitting in the train, with Paris getting nearer, and Switzerland with all its dangers, the Switzerland of the past week, slowly fading farther and farther into the background. My parents were living in Paris now, and so were my brother, Hans, and his wife, Eva; they had just recently married.

For a few days we slept on the floor of my parents' tiny one-room apartment. In Hans's and Eva's *logement* (hardly a room, it was more like a cubicle) there was no space to share. I was prepared for the fact that an emigrant's life in Paris would be no bowl of cherries; it had often been portrayed to us in very stark terms by emigrants who had spent some time there, but I was shocked when I saw the reality. Still, it did us good to spend a few days together with my family and just talk about things.

Hans had kept up a correspondence with friends who had fled earlier to Amsterdam. Hermann and Elli repeatedly wrote that they hoped we would follow them there. They gave us to understand that people were needed in Holland, people who had experience and could help organize the border work. They would be able to provide us with a place to stay.

We knew that Holland was not an easy place for emigrants like us—it was one of the countries where the dangers were greatest. The Dutch

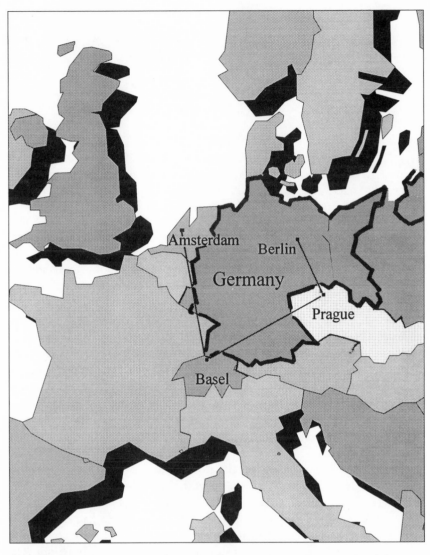

*The Gestapo was closing in on us and we fled from Basel to Amsterdam. All the while, Hitler was stepping up expansionist pressure on his neighbors and continuing an ominous military buildup. Other governments did nothing to stop him; they still believed they could achieve "peace in our time."*

government sent illegal refugees arrested on Dutch territory directly across the border into Germany, directly into the hands of the Gestapo. We had to be especially careful.

We were uneasy about crossing the Dutch border with our forged passports, but we made it. Some time before, in order to be prepared for any eventuality, Hans had gotten passports from a Zurich couple our age and had our photos perfectly mounted in place of theirs. And so I now stood in the large cold room, with the gray housecat Grijsje lying at my feet, turning myself in front of the fireplace when I got too hot in front or too cold in back. Hans had gone north to Groningen to meet people who were sending materials across the border there.

Through Elli and Hermann we had found lodging with a theater couple. They were cheerful and friendly people, but they often found themselves without work because they were known to be all too liberal. Still, whatever there was to eat they shared with us.

Our hosts spoke no German, and at first it was difficult to make ourselves understood. It was easier for me than for Hans, because I had quickly been able to slip back into the language I had spoken for a year when I was about ten years old. Back then, as part of a throng of hungry Viennese children, I had been sent to Holland, where a family in Apeldoorn took on the responsibility of fattening me up. It was months before "Zuster," my Dutch mother, discovered that I had forgotten my native language. And how important it was now that I have no German accent when I speak Dutch! Hans never said a word out on the streets. When something had to be said, I was the one who spoke. If we needed cough drops, I requested them from the pharmacist. Whenever we wanted to sit in a café, I ordered the coffee. And even at the fish shop it was I, not Hans, who bought the matjes herring. It was a strange life. We were cut off from everything, we knew very few people, and as few as possible were to know us. Sometimes one or another of our friends dropped by—Hermann and Elli, for example—and then we could speak freely, talking about whatever we chose to discuss without having to whisper or make sure that we were not overheard.

I was often alone. Hans would go to the border area for days at a time, staying in various towns. There were new contacts and drop-off sites, literature was sent across the border, and refugees were helped to escape. People there accepted him as if he were an old friend. They wanted to help, and he felt safe with them—as safe as anyone in our position could feel in Holland. While he was away I was the central contact for people who came from the border area to Amsterdam.

Sometimes I felt lonely. Hans was at the border and I understood very clearly what kind of danger he faced. I thought: for years I have dreamed of simply doing things that are part of living a normal life; now I have the time, but I am alone—the only company I have is Grijsje, the gray tom cat, rubbing up against my ankles. Still, I enjoyed walking through the city, and I often spent entire days wandering along the canals through the old sections of Amsterdam. Sometimes our theater couple gave me a pass to the Concertgebouw. Most of all I enjoyed spending time in the Rijksmuseum. I read a lot—something I hadn't been able to do for years in our hectic life. I felt a desire to write. Mostly I wrote about life as an emigrant and as an illegal refugee, and about the struggle against the barbarous regime. Sometimes I kept a journal, because I wanted to describe things as they really were. Or, let's say, as I saw them. Every detail had to be captured. I didn't know if anything I wrote would ever be published, but at the time it just didn't matter. Maybe later, after our hopes had been realized. . . .

Whenever Hans came home he was tired and restless. He was not able to relax.

"Tell me what's been happening," he would say.

"Here?" I said. "Nothing's happening here."

"No matter, tell me something—anything. Tell me something about everyday life, something trivial and amusing that I won't have to think about. I just want to hear your voice, it does me good."

But things didn't work out that way. There was so much that couldn't be suppressed. How could we not think about events? Even though we were isolated here and knew very little about what was going on in the world, other than what we read in the daily newspaper? When one or another of our friends dropped by, when we were among ourselves and started to talk, the discussions never ended.

The setbacks in the Spanish Civil War. Was the news true? A poem by Jef Last that I had read in a Dutch newspaper kept coming to mind:

> . . . but for the flame in our hearts,
> We could not have endured the cold.

The trials in Moscow . . . we ask ourselves how this can be happening and we cannot find an answer. Can we remain silent? What does this mean for us? "We can't afford to keep banging our heads against the wall because of what they're doing in Moscow," Hermann said.

"You think we should act as if it simply doesn't concern us?"

"Don't we have enough problems of our own?"

Oh, how long were we going to have to carry on? It was almost five years . . . still, no matter what happened, we would never stop resisting.

And the danger of war grew. Would we be able to stop it?

I was reminded of Apeldoorn again and again; it was only a few hours from here by train. I would so have loved to visit the house in the woods again, with its rose garden in front and the gravel path all around. The vegetable and fruit garden behind the house, where I had picked such large strawberries, and later in summer, deeper in the woods, blueberries. The wide stretches of heath I loved to wander through, hours on end. And Zuster, who had to be a very old woman now. Only a few hours away!

"I've been trying to think of how we might do it without making a big mistake," said Hans. "But I just can't come up with a way. Just think, we don't even have a name we can use there! And all the questions you know she would ask. Maybe later, at a more appropriate time. . . ."

"Apeldoorn" had been printed on the tag they put around my neck at the train station in Vienna. That was 1919, shortly after the war. My mother had spent the entire evening and half the night before washing my hair. Afterwards my hair smelled like petroleum and she had to rinse it over and over again to get out the scent. I had never had lice, but apparently you could very easily get them in school, especially with thick, curly hair like mine. I wanted to know why now, at this particular time, and Marie, who was from Upper Austria, said, "It's because of the war."

Everything happened because of the war.

The next day's lice examination was awful. If anything looked suspicious, a child's hair was cut very short. If a lice colony was actually found, the child was shorn and had something poured over his bald head. The mothers of these shaved heads all claimed that the lice diagnosis must have been a mistake. Nothing was found on my head, but I was terribly frightened when the lice commission spent a long time sniffing through my hair before deciding not to cut it off.

To escape the famine in Vienna, the hungry Viennese children were taken to neutral countries on chartered trains. We were told that there was more than enough to eat in these countries, and that the people there wanted to take us in before we got sick from malnutrition. That's why my brother was sent to Denmark, my cousin to Sweden, and I to Holland.

The trains were very slow, we were on board for three days and nights. I had a window seat and slept a lot. Once I woke up and saw a glowing chimney through the window. It was incredibly tall and appeared to grow until it touched the heavens. It glowed brighter and brighter, yellow and red, brighter than anything I had ever seen, and it seemed to me that our train was traveling around the chimney in circles. Then it began to sway, and I was happy it was so far away from us. Then it happened: the glowing chimney buckled and fell, crashing to the ground along its entire length. It had been very exciting, and I remember thinking: My parents stayed behind in Vienna and I'm going somewhere farther and farther away. . . . Whom can I tell about what I've just seen? and I started to cry. A couple of adults came to comfort me, saying: Of course, she fell asleep and had a bad dream. And one said: She's homesick.

At the station in Apeldoorn there was some sort of committee, along with a group of boy scouts, waiting for us. The scouts took us to our foster homes. They were much older than we, probably sixteen or seventeen, and they all had bicycles. My boy scout spoke no German. He set me on the crossbar in front of him. I had never sat on a crossbar before, and I was afraid we would fall over along with his bicycle. The crossbar cut into my flesh and bones. It was a long ride because the house was outside the city, and I was in pain, sliding around on the bar; I wanted to change my seat, but my boy scout didn't understand me. It seemed to me that he wasn't entirely comfortable either.

By the time we finally arrived at the house on the edge of the woods, it was almost dark. A house with a dark forest behind it! The woman who welcomed me spoke German. That was somewhat reassuring. She said I should call her Zuster; that meant "nurse," and she was a nurse. There were several other children there too, and they all called her Zuster. She explained that they were Dutch children who had been sent to her house on the edge of the forest for rest and recuperation, and she had offered to take one of the Viennese children too. I was that child. But my recovery was a slow affair. At first Zuster gave me some soup that tasted like warm water. She explained that the doctor had prescribed a ten-day diet of thin soup for the Viennese children, because after a long period of hunger their stomachs could not tolerate any fat.

We were supposed to stay three months to be fattened up. I actually did gain some weight, but Zuster wrote to my parents in Vienna telling them that three months was not long enough and, unless I extended my stay, I would soon lose the weight I had gained. After much hemming and hawing, my parents agreed, knowing there was still very little to eat in Vienna. In the meantime, I had learned Dutch from the other children, was sent to school, and forgot my German. At school I sang along:

*Wilhelmus van Nassouwe*
*Ben ick van Duytschen bloet . . .*

(William of Nassau
I am of German blood . . .)

I stayed an entire year and was no longer so very pale and skinny when I was sent back to Vienna.

I think that must have been 1920. And this was 1938. I knew it would be dangerous to show up in Apeldoorn now, with my forged papers, as an illegal emigrant, with an illegal husband. I just couldn't do it. I couldn't visit Zuster in her house by the forest.

Even today this makes me sad.

When the tulips blossomed I persuaded Hans to go with me to Haarlem. There, among the throngs of visitors, it would certainly be no more dangerous than in Amsterdam. We spent an entire wonderful day in this shimmering world of flowers. We had heard about the tulips, but what we saw, the endless fields of color, was something we would never have been able to imagine. And it was such a joy simply to get out of the city into the open air, simply to be somewhere else.

It was already late when we got back home. A friend from the border was waiting for us.

"Several of our contacts over there have been arrested. You'll have to get out of here immediately."

# PARIS

I knew Paris. The exciting city I loved so much since the time—it was now almost ten years ago—I had studied there. Montparnasse, the charming little hotel in rue de la Gaîté, the courses and lectures on boulevard Raspail, the student cafés—it was all still there. Yet it had nothing to do with the Paris I now found—in the year 1938—a city swarming with German emigrants, full of people who were looking for work but had no work permits, people who were searching for a new existence but did not even have a residence permit. This was a Paris I didn't know.

We found our first job through the Emigrant Aid Committee. We were told it was a rare stroke of good luck that they had been able to find something for us so quickly. A job you could wriggle your way into without a permit—that's what everyone was looking for. For us normal emigrants it was impossible to get a *carte de travail*. That's why we were so lucky, they said, that they had gotten a request for a married couple, room and board included.

We were being sent to a Herr Böhm. He was an emigrant from Munich, where he had owned a fine-arts printing business, and had now set up shop in Paris. He was looking for a couple to run his household and take care of his two sons, one ten, one fifteen years of age. His wife was spending a year in America with her uncle, a piece of information that at the time gave me cause to wonder.

Herr Böhm said there was actually very little to do, and running the household was hardly enough to keep me occupied. In the meantime, Hans was to address envelopes for a direct-mail business, approximately one thousand per day.

"One thousand addresses?" Hans protested. "You have to be kidding! And what would we get for this slave work?"

"Well, lodging and meals, of course," replied Herr Böhm. After all, he would have to recover his costs somehow, if he was going to be this generous with two new emigrants.

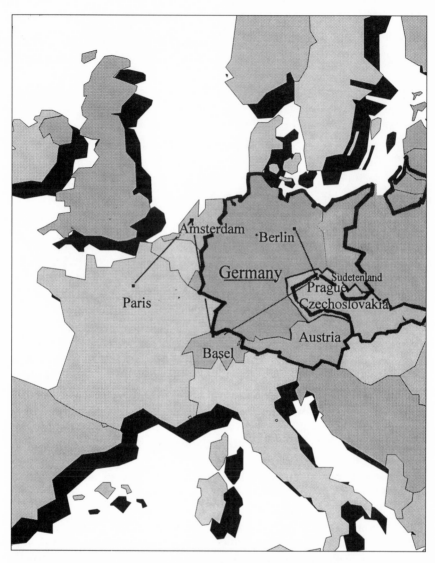

*Holland soon became too dangerous for us and we left for Paris. From there, in quick succession, we witnessed the annexation of Austria in March 1938, the annexation of the Sudetenland in October of the same year; and by the spring of 1939 the German army had occupied all of Czechoslovakia.*

Our so-called "lodging" was little more than a storeroom, and we had great difficulty opening a path to the bed. There was no bedding anywhere.

Herr Böhm himself did the daily shopping for the household. Every day he came home with ground meat and herring: 350 grams of meat and two-thirds of a loaf of bread. Every day, always precisely the same thing because, it seemed, there was nothing else he could eat. Our evening meal consisted of nothing but smoked herring and bread. Herr Böhm served each of us, and always, before deboning the fish, he held it up by its tail and said, "A lovely herring, a lovely herring!"

Hans found the whole situation ridiculous and immediately wanted to give notice and quit. I would have liked to stay a few days longer. Where were we going to go? This was all we had. Neither my parents nor my brother had any space for us.

But Hans had lost all patience, and he told Herr Böhm that we would be moving out that very day. We would not let ourselves be exploited like this—the thousand addresses per day he wanted to squeeze out of us, the meat loaf that was not meat, the tiny room that wasn't a room. When Hans went on to mention the "lovely herring," Herr Böhm got awfully angry. He bent over in pain, complaining about his gall bladder, and claimed it was all our fault. He was helpless and alone, with two children and no wife; he had had to send her to America, she had been so overwrought lately. I understood only too well how this might have come about. An acquaintance of Herr Böhm's happened to come by just then, heard what was going on, and said, "I told you so, I told you no one would take that, you stupid ass."

That was the end of our first job in Paris.

What were we to do now? Luckily a few Spandauers had shown up in the meantime. As always, they were ready to help. Otto B. let us spend a few nights on the floor of his tiny hotel room. We had to sneak in past the concierge. Ewald, who had left Switzerland before us, was also there. He and his wife, Mia, worked for a French family and lived in the same building in a *logement*—that is, a small room for domestic help located on the top floor. Ewald knew that the *logement* next to theirs was vacant. We had to come home after midnight to keep from being seen. We never used the main stairway either. Instead, we climbed a steep set of stairs that went up the outside wall, every night clambering up nine flights of stairs to our secret shelter. It was hard for me, but whenever I got out of breath Hans gave me a push from behind.

A relative of the family for whom Ewald worked had a clinic. He needed someone to clean, stoke the basement furnace, and take care of everything else that could be considered the job of a janitorial couple. He led us around the clinic and explained the work, informing us along the way that Hans would also have to destroy the laboratory animals, the guinea pigs, after they had been injected with one thing or another. Hans refused: he wouldn't kill guinea pigs. So the clinic director decided to leave the guinea-pig work to the concierge next door and deduct the amount he was paid from our salary. He wouldn't be able to pay all that much anyway. Emigrants did not receive high salaries; it was, after all, a risk to hire them. Still, there was an empty room for us in the clinic.

The room really was empty, containing nothing but a bed. But—even the bed was empty: no blankets, no pillows, no sheets. Only a mattress. When Hans asked the owner for bedding, he replied that he had promised nothing more than a room with a bed. I calmed Hans down, assuring him that we could cover up with our coats until we were able to get what bedding we needed. And for the time being we would simply have to use our suitcase as a pillow. What else were we to do?

The clinic was located in a better part of the city and looked quite imposing: a stately entrance hall made entirely of marble, and the owner himself was very elegant. We scrubbed all the time, working especially hard to keep the marble floor clean. A receptionist as elegant as the building itself trailed after us, her high heels clicking across the marble floor, in search of spots we had not adequately attacked with our brushes. We never found out what kind of clinic this was. Most of the patients were women and the treatment was quite secretive; it certainly had something to do with cosmetics, because many of the rooms were covered with paraffin—which could only be removed by rigorous scrubbing and scraping after it had dried and hardened. Scrubbing and scraping all day, sleeping all night with my head resting on the hard corners and edges of my suitcase—it was worse than I had imagined it would be. Already the first night, I pushed the suitcase off of the bed because it had given me an awful headache. Hans didn't want anything under his head either; anyway, he produced a frightful snore whenever he rested his head on the suitcase.

Evenings we went down to the basement to stoke the furnace, and the next-door concierge often came by to chat with us. He was a nice, friendly man who hoped, as he often told us, that we foreigners were not being too badly exploited and that, personally, he had nothing against emigrants, especially not against us; we were, after all, his friends. But it certainly was expecting a lot that on top of everything else we were to stoke the furnace only because our boss was too cheap to leave the heating to him, the next-door concierge, and pay him a reasonable salary for it. Not that he was envious, he said, not that he, a Frenchman, disliked foreigners. . . .

"What a fool!" Hans said afterward. "Poor, deluded fool. He lets himself be convinced that we emigrants are taking something away from him and doesn't see that we're actually being pitted against each other."

About two weeks later the lady with the high heels found another spot on the marble floor of the hallway. She went to Hans, grabbed for the scrub brush in his hand, and said, "I'll show you how you. . . ."

"I'd like to show you something too," I heard Hans say. I turned around only to see the scrub brush sailing down the length of the hallway.

That was the end of our second job in Paris.

My brother introduced me to a number of his colleagues. There was a young physicist's family, including a baby, and they needed someone to take the baby to the park twice a day, for two hours at a time. The child was charming, and I was happy to take little Irene to the lovely Parc de Montsouris. Even if you couldn't live on the money you made for taking such a stroll through the park, this kind of job was still one of the most sought-after among emigrant women, because you were never asked for your work permit. The only unpleasant aspect of my time with Irene was the result of her mother's insistence that, on every walk she took, she was to eat a banana, bananas then being considered the basis of good nutrition. But Irene started to scream every time she saw me take one of those detestable bananas out of my bag. And the more I tried to persuade her, the louder she screamed. I'm sure she has never forgiven me, not to this very day.

Edmund, who had also come to Paris from Basel, was trying to set up a decorating business with a few friends. They got work painting the apartments of emigrants who were already longtime residents of Paris. They asked Hans to work with them. He tried a few times, but things just didn't work out; the apartment owners were always getting angry because they felt the work wasn't progressing fast enough. When the owners grew impatient and wanted to find out what was taking so long, they more often than not found their work brigade energetically engaged in political discourse. They were arguing about the Moscow Trials, about the role of the POUM in the Spanish Civil War, Léon Blum's politics, or Germany's war preparations. On this particular day the apartment owner looked in on them, the painters were discussing the tactical mistakes of the Popular Front. In the meantime, paint from the half-finished walls was dripping onto the floor; one of the painters was standing on a ladder waving his brush in the air to emphasize his theory; another was lying stretched out on the floor reading an article out loud to the whole assembly. Naturally, the apartment owner did not want to pay. Hans soon saw that there was no point in trying to work with such strategists. So he looked around for small projects he could do on his own, like repairs or washing windows. But finding this kind of work was always a matter of luck.

Sometimes I found work as a household helper; that's what most emigrant women did. But there were many times when neither Hans nor I could find a job. Our greatest concern was finding enough money to pay our weekly rent. We had moved into one of the cheap little hotels on the rue de Plaisance in the fourteenth arrondissement, a room with a two-burner gas cooker in the corner. Many of the people we knew lived in hotel rooms like this; there were many little hotels in the fourteenth arrondissement: primitive, not particularly clean, but cheap. We gave each other the addresses of these hotels, because we all felt most comfortable living in areas where other emigrants lived too. But no matter where we found shelter, rent had to be paid. Otherwise we'd be thrown out. And if you had found no work that week you had to look around for friends who might be able to lend you some money.

Finally, that's why we decided—along with my parents—to take another stab at the most common occupation for emigrants: writing addresses for mail-order businesses. The pay was miserable, but you could expect reasonably steady employment. A few emigrants had arrived with enough money to set up businesses like these. Through newspaper ads, mostly in the provinces, they sold diamond rings, gold watches, and all kinds of jewelry at dirt-cheap prices, everything genuinely "semiauthentic." The replies to the ads were passed on to the emigrants, who worked at home writing out the addresses for the shipments. The orders were filled and sent off C.O.D. In addition to the articles the customer had ordered, the packages also contained a surprise which, more often than not, was of some value. Most of the customers agreed to pay for the shipping; if they didn't, they would receive nothing at all.

In spite of the miserable salary, we did manage to earn enough to pay for the most basic of necessities. Still, I can remember bad days, days on which my parents ran out of money, when there wasn't a crumb of bread in the house. I can still see my father in front of me, how he—punctually, as always—sat down at his old typewriter at seven o'clock in the morning and started banging out addresses, a red plaid blanket wrapped around his knees, because now he was always cold. Then, in the evening, he regularly worked on his book for two and a half hours. He had begun writing it when he emigrated, and a Viennese publisher had expressed some interest.

My father had long ago given up the hope of working with his previous business contacts to create a new life for his family. It had slowly become clear to him that these contacts were no longer there, that he could not build any kind of normal existence: he was a Jew, he had become persona non grata.

My parents moved. In place of their dark little hole near the avenue Emile Zola, they had found an apartment in a suburb south of Paris, in Chatenay-Malabry. It was a new development, the garden town of Butte Rouge. The town had a socialist government. Since Butte Rouge was forty-five minutes away from Paris, there were still some vacant apartments. Rents were low, and the small apartments were quite pretty and pleasantly located on the edge of a forest. A number of German emigrants had already moved in. People said that, even if you were late with your rent from time to time, you didn't really have to worry because the buildings were not privately owned, and the local authorities showed an understanding of the emigrants' situation. So now, once every week, my father took the bus into Paris to deliver his packages and envelopes and to pick up new work.

Through an acquaintance my mother got work from a Paris fashion house that gave out piecework to emigrant women. She sewed elegant and expensive clothing, crocheted dresses and suits from silk ribbons, everything to order, and her work was much admired. But her salary was the same low emigrant pay: just enough to cover the cost of daily purchases such as bread, milk, and potatoes.

The owner of the mail-order business Hans and I worked for had once been a member of the Prussian parliament. And for our stinking little salaries Hans and I had to spend our days typing, from early in the morning until late into the evening. But at least we had work.

Soon we also moved to Butte Rouge, into an apartment in the same building where my parents lived, one floor directly below theirs; it was cheaper and prettier than the dirty little hotels in the fourteenth arrondissement. I would have dearly loved to enjoy the forest, but there wasn't time even for a short walk. We never left the table Hans had built, we just sat there tirelessly typing addresses.

Sometimes I was able to find more interesting work. Writers, journalists, and filmmakers who had fled Germany needed someone to type their manuscripts. Naturally, this was more pleasant than typing those despicable envelopes, but I soon learned that my pay was always at risk. These people, whose names were known to everyone in the Weimar Republic, surely hadn't intended to cheat me. But it happened again and again. They weren't able to sell their manuscripts, they had to put off paying me, and finally they just forgot. Once more I had worked for nothing.

My brother and his wife had been in Paris for some time. At first, Eva stayed behind in Berlin and carried on resistance work with a group of students at the university. They produced and distributed literature opposing the national socialists. Hans was already in Paris and was making preparations for Eva to follow. But before he could finish his arrangements Eva was also forced to flee. It was one of those cases of misunderstanding, confusion, mistrust, and suspicion that arise in such troubled circumstances and cause great damage. Two students who were working for another resistance group had been arrested. In all the ensuing confusion, friends of both arrested students had become convinced that people from Eva's group had denounced them to the Gestapo. The two groups were both antifascist, but they had some political differences.

Was it panic? Was it hatred for everyone in the struggle against national socialism who didn't share their own convictions? What could possibly have led people within the Resistance to such absurd conclusions, such irresponsible actions?

They apparently believed they could protect themselves from further arrests by threatening Eva. She was warned that if there were any more arrests of members from their group, they would be forced to assume that Eva, or members of her group, had denounced their friends. To make their point, they would inform the Gestapo of Eva's activities.

It is not possible to hold a reasonable discussion with insane people. My brother immediately went back to Berlin, despite the risk to himself, to get Eva out. By marrying Hans, as was already planned, she would obtain an Austrian passport and would be allowed to leave Germany legally. Eva's father valued good manners, no matter what the circumstances, so Hans, as was only fitting, was invited to dinner. Already walking on hot coals, he asked for the hand of Herr Rosenthal's daughter during the soup course, and Herr Rosenthal concurred, in spite of the unseemly giggles of the bride to be. That evening, a few family members were hastily assembled to celebrate the marriage: Herr Rosenthal and several Jewish relatives, and his wife, Stella, with the aryan, in part aristocratic, branch of the family. Someone took a snapshot: no one knew that this would be the last picture of an old Berlin family at home on the Bayrischen Platz. The next morning the civil ceremony took place at City Hall, and the couple then rushed to the Austrian consulate to get Eva's new passport. One day later, they left the Third Reich for Paris. With Austrian passports they were able to enter France without a visa.

Eva took a job with the famous photographer Philip Halsman; before leaving Germany he had been falsely accused of murder. At any rate, he hired Eva to assist him in his studio and taught her how to retouch photographs. She also cleaned his apartment and prepared his meals. Some time later, Hans received a small scholarship from the Sorbonne so that he could continue his work in physics. And finally Eva was able to find temporary work in a research institute.

The majority of emigrants who had been in Paris for any length of time were able to overcome their most pressing problems with papers, even if this meant nothing more than another extension of their residence permits. As new arrivals, however, we were always being summoned to the central police station, making one application after another. And we had to content ourselves with no more than a promise that our applications would soon be processed. Until we had our papers we were not *en ordre*, not legal. To become *en ordre* you needed passport photos, copies of birth certificates, and all sorts of other documents that most of us did not have.

Near the Madeleine there was a studio called Photo Dorit, where most of the emigrants had their photos and photocopies made. The owner was a German emigrant himself, and he had set his prices to attract emigrant business. He was also an excellent photographer. Hans soon discovered that the photographer was none other than his former mentor, Franz Pfemfert.

"I've been thinking it over," Hans said to me, "I'm going to go and talk to Franz." He asked if I'd like to go with him, and I suggested that it might be better for him to go alone first, to see how Franz reacted. I had never met the Pfemferts in person and knew about them only through all the stories I had heard from Hans. For many years in Berlin, where Franz had been the publisher of *Die Aktion*, they had been close friends. Franz Pfemfert had shown a great interest in the young Hans Fittko, and had guided him into a journalistic career and introduced him into the broader circle of Expressionists around the magazine. Some sixty years later, Pfemfert's niece Nina wrote to me about this period:

"In my youth I felt the heavy burden of politics and culture in the *Aktion* milieu. Uncle Franz and Aunt Anja were a very authoritarian family, while for me Hans Fittko was always a calm harbor in the midst of the Pfemfert chaos."

Over the course of some years Hans had distanced himself from the Pfemferts' political opinions. Franz's intolerance toward those who differed from him politically was well known. In this case, Franz seemed to consider Hans's development as something of a personal insult as well; Franz and Anja had both looked upon him more or less as an adopted son. For them, Hans's changing political views was pure treason. Franz then abruptly broke off the relationship, and they had not talked to each other since.

Franz had always shown both a great enthusiasm and a talent for photography. And now, with their studio at the Madeleine, he and Anja had managed to build up a modest existence for themselves. In addition to the emigrants, famous French intellectuals as well as celebrated exiles from the Weimar Republic all came to Photo Dorit to have their portraits made. In the waiting room of the studio hung the most striking portrait of André Gide I have ever seen.

In the meantime, Franz had completely given up all his political activities, including publishing, and had changed in many ways. He wanted no contact with the various political groups among the emigrants. He received Hans as if they had never had a parting of ways. I showed myself to be of great value to the Pfemferts in that I often rescued meals that Anja regularly burnt. She was an excellent translator but had never become a cook.

Franz had changed so much that now he even had a pet cat by the name of Minka. It was common knowledge that the friendship between Franz Pfemfert and Rosa Luxemburg had fallen into temporary disrepair after Franz had booted her cat off the sofa. These days he wrote odes to Minka, praising her beauty and grace, and her spirit. In the evening he often read the cat poems to us.

Minka was basically a lovely cat, but she ate only liver. Not just any liver, but *foie de génisse*, veal liver. Now on Tuesdays, delicatessens were closed. Of course Franz bought two slices of liver on Mondays, but when he took the second slice out of the refrigerator on Tuesdays and gave it to the cat, Minka refused to eat it. So every Tuesday, Franz, unbeknownst to

Minka, took the second slice of liver out of the refrigerator, put it into his pocket, and stole out of the apartment. Only when he returned ten minutes later, setting his packet down on the table, was Minka ready to believe that he had bought the liver fresh. And this is how emigration had changed the fierce polemicist Franz Pfemfert.

Hans and I had not joined any of the numerous opposition groups in Paris, either. We had a circle of old friends who—like us—kept their distance from the various organizations; we found the atmosphere of political turf battles, of the often bitter internal struggles among groups and splinter groups, unbearable. On the borders, where we had spent the majority of our time in emigration, we had always stayed in contact with resistance groups inside Germany. No one was interested in party membership there; we all worked together. Sometimes we felt ourselves isolated from the centers of emigration, where there must have been thorough analyses of the political situation in Europe. Now we were here in Paris. There was a lot of talk here; but the struggle against fascism in our country seemed to have deteriorated into endless quarreling. Even among the courageous soldiers of the Spanish Civil War there were bitter feuds. This factional fighting reminded us very much of the fights among leftists before 1933—it almost seemed as if nothing had happened since then. Now people were arguing about the strategy for the Popular Front in the same way they had earlier argued about the United Front, "from below or from above." At the insistence of friends I went to a meeting of the German faction of French unions. I wanted to see what changes the Popular Front had made. Had the antifascists made any progress in finding a way to unite? But at the meeting, I found the same segregated groups as before. They were still damning each other and blaming each other for the split. It seemed to me that many were the same unreconstructed dogmatists I had known, and that they were still beating each other over the head about anything one or the other might have said at any time in the past.

At the Parisian Day of Humanity, in Garches, we met up with friends from over there. Isn't that Fanny? She turned briefly toward me and walked on.

"Fanny . . . what's going on?" I stepped in front of her.

"I'm not interested in having anything more to do with you. I heard that you've become Trotskyites."

"You hear lots of things here, most of them lies." I was furious. "That we're Trotskyites is pure fantasy. And even if it were true, then I can only conclude that you ought to mind your own business. How could this possibly be reason enough to discard old friends and comrades? Don't you know what solidarity means? This stupid, ugly pettiness, is that your contribution to the struggle against the Nazis?"

One evening, shortly after this encounter, we had a terrible blowup with our friend Rolf. We were sitting together talking with him. They beat up Herbert L., Rolf said, and he was found lying on the ground, bleeding and half-conscious, near the Bastille. They knocked his teeth out.

That can't be! I yelled. Another rumor. Who could possibly have done it? Why? Herbert . . . one of our bravest, said Rolf's wife, Erna.

"But why has he split with his party here in Paris?" said Rolf. "You weren't here then. What happened in Spain when he stopped holding to the political line, he and a lot of others, you didn't hear about that, you were working somewhere else—you don't know anything about the Spanish experiences that some of us had. And now you find it hard to believe that some of his old comrades might mug him! Man, just ask them . . . just ask him! You're so damned naive. How long have you been here in Paris, anyway? Apparently there's a lot you don't understand. You've got a lot more surprises coming. Why? Because everything is different now. Because things haven't turned out the way we expected them to turn out. And maybe it's because there are some problems that simply cannot be solved. But that is no justification for using violence against our own comrades!"

"Rolf," I said, shocked, "do you mean to say that attacks on comrades are happening all the time? Do you believe that our friends who suffered together in torture chambers, fought together on the Spanish front, are now fighting each other like mortal enemies whenever they have a difference of opinion? The fearless are fighting among themselves? Because they have different opinions, so we're told, and that's why it's inevitable? And these are the people whose convictions were once more important to them than their lives. Where can this be leading us?"

One day Hans came back from the city with a bundle of work more voluminous than usual. As if to order, because we had reached a point where every one of our revenue sources seemed to have dried up; there weren't even enough addresses to type. My parents didn't have enough work either, and they were running out of money. The job Hans brought with him that evening was from an exclusive perfume house: they needed 135 letters to private clients typed on elegant beige letterhead, and no erasures were allowed. The job was to be completed and delivered to their Paris offices by ten o'clock the following morning. Hans had agreed because he was sure I could do it. Of course, it meant that I would be typing all night.

As morning approached, I was getting hungry. Hans was asleep and I didn't want to wake him. But I couldn't afford to lose the time it would take to cook something for myself. There was no bread in the house. At seven o'clock I heard my mother's footsteps coming from their apartment and I went up.

"I'm hungry, mother," I said. "Do you have anything I can eat in a hurry? Like a roll? I'm in a real rush."

She gave me two slices of bread and some salami. "Don't devour it like that!" she admonished. "You'll get a stomachache."

I went downstairs and continued to type. And I did get a stomachache. I kept typing. But more slowly all the time. Until I just couldn't hit another key.

Hans went upstairs and got my mother. "She needs a doctor," I heard her say. But how could we pay a doctor? We didn't have a *centime*.

Like all emigrants who got sick, we had to call in one of the German doctors who were not allowed to practice in France. Across the street there was a young doctor from Frankfurt. Hans called him, and he gave me a laxative, and morphine to kill the searing pain. He was too young to know that this was the wrong treatment. My pain got worse. My father took the bus into the city and, with the help of my brother, found two emigrant doctors both of whom had good reputations: Fritz Fränkel and Minna Flake. They had a car, so they all drove back together to Butte Rouge. They were both of the opinion that my appendix might have ruptured and that I would have to be operated on immediately. "Every minute counts," said Minna. They couldn't take me to the hospital because they had no license to practice; if they were caught treating a patient, they would be arrested.

Someone found a taxi; someone found a hospital; someone found a surgeon. I can remember the trip from the southern suburb of Chatenay-Malabry to the new Hôpital Beaujon in the northern suburb of Clichy, across Paris, over every existing cobblestone street in the city. I lay down in the back seat and Hans held me, because the doctors had said I shouldn't move. At the hospital I first had to answer a barrage of questions. When I couldn't think of an answer, the doctors urged me on, telling me my life was hanging in the balance! Which at this point didn't matter much to me, the pain was simply too excruciating.

By the time I was released from my six-week stay in the hospital, Austria had been annexed to the German Reich.

# SPAIN. THE SUDETENLAND.
# MUNICH. THE PACT

$M$ost of our relatives were living in Vienna. Who had not gotten out? Who had been able to escape?

We saw pictures of the jubilation when the Nazis marched into Vienna; we read about the mistreatment of the Jews. I was horrified, but I wasn't really surprised. I recalled the disparaging cant of my teacher at the elementary school on Schönbrunner Strasse.

"Mama, what is characteristic Jewish trading mentality?" I asked when I got home.

"Where did you ever hear that?" my mother wanted to know.

"My teacher gave a lecture about it. She said that I was a good example of it. Because I gave my friend my pink notebook, and she gave me a little mirror for it."

My mother's sister, the Viennese painter Malva Schalek, had always been very close to me. She had been able to flee Vienna and reach her brother in Leitmeritz. She took her old aunt with her. Otherwise Aunt Emma would have been left behind, alone in Vienna. Now, at least, they were both safe. But were they really safe in the Sudetenland?

Where could anyone be safe?

My sister-in-law Eva was expecting a child. I admired her. Under these circumstances, in these times! "Where did you ever find the courage?" I asked her. "I want a child," she said. "It's as simple as that. We both have jobs now. Things will have to work out somehow."

Once more I started talking to Hans about having children. "Just look," I said. "They're not afraid of bringing a baby into the world, horrible as this world may be." But Hans was firm.

133

"No, we can't, not now. They won't have an easy time of it either, even though they both have professions they can practice and they're earning a living—modest as it is. But for us it would be an irresponsible thing to do, to have a child when we ourselves often have nothing to eat. In this world where war has become inevitable. And no matter what happens: as long as Germany is in the grips of fascism, we'll continue to fight—and it's open season on us! How can we have children now?"

*My aunt Malva Schalek (left) and my mother, Jula Ekstein (right), Vienna, ca. 1934*

I knew he was right. I consoled myself with hopes for the future; things would change when the Terror was past, and we would be able to go home.

But there was no real hope of an early return home. Germany was bombing republican Spain. London and Paris persisted in a policy of "nonintervention." Hitler's war preparations were unmistakable. Against an eastern front? Against a western front? France and England "appeased" him at every turn. Good relations had to be maintained. They would give in, a little more each time. The character of the Nazi regime seemed to pose no problem for them.

German political emigrants warned of the consequences of pursuing such a policy. As a result, we were condemned as warmongers who were undermining attempts to stay on good terms with Hitler and thus avoid conflict. For that reason we were considered undesirable. We were held in suspicion.

Eva's daughter, Catherine, was born in the middle of the Sudeten crisis. When Hitler demanded this part of Czechoslovakia, people in France were gripped by apprehension and anxiety. I was taking the bus home, the line from Porte d'Orléans to Butte Rouge. When we stopped in one town I saw white placards on the wall. The bus passengers stood up and stared out the windows. It was a long text, but I only saw one word: MOBILISA-TION. I felt woozy. I heard the other passengers talking among themselves: "No war! Anything but war! Anything else but war! It's no business of ours, *les Sudètes!*" And, sure enough, a few days later "agreement" was reached in Munich. The Führer had been appeased, and France breathed a sigh of relief.

One morning, after my mother had come home with bread from the bakery, she went into the kitchen to make coffee. I noticed that she was crying. "What's wrong, mother?" I asked, shocked at her tears. "What happened?" She told me that the baker's wife had shouted excitedly: "They signed! There'll be peace! *C'est la paix!*" and that someone in the shop had chimed in: "Long live peace! *Vive la paix!*" and then the others laughed nervously and sobbed: "*Vive la paix! Vive la paix!*"

A few days later the Wehrmacht began marching into Czechoslovakia and occupied the Sudetenland.

Malva Schalek fled from Leitmeritz to Prague with Aunt Emma. Accompanying them was her brother, the chief federal magistrate.

Not half a year later, we sat around the radio in Butte Rouge and listened to the news: The Wehrmacht now occupied all of Bohemia and

Moravia; they marched into Prague. There was nowhere Malva Schalek, her aunt, and her brother could flee to.

Life in Paris became especially hard. Something had gone wrong with the mail-order business and we had no work. We hadn't paid the rent for two months. My parents barely had enough for even the most basic necessities. Not even my brother could help. We had to try something else.

I heard about a family who was looking for household help—Americans who wanted to spend the summer in France and had leased a house near Paris. They were looking for an emigrant who would come to live with them until fall, to keep house and take care of the child from time to time when the parents traveled.

Arrangements of this sort were not uncommon among emigrants. Up to this point Hans and I had been able to avoid taking work that would require us to live apart. But everything was so difficult now, maybe this— at least for a short time—was a solution? Hans had an acquaintance in the suburb of Ivry, and for very little money he could share a room there, just for the time being, of course. In the meantime, my brother, along with Eva and their little daughter Catherine, would take over our apartment. Then my mother could take care of Catherine during the day, and Eva would be able to accept a position at the institute where Hans was already employed.

It was difficult for us to follow through with this plan. We had always been so certain that we would not let ourselves be parted, not under any circumstances. But when you cannot pay the rent, when you do not even have enough money for crumbs, the pressure becomes too great. The friends who had told us about the job with the American family encouraged us: they were nice people, and I would get along well with them; they were interested in politics; they were cultured.

Finally, Hans and I decided to go to Marne-la-Coquette where the Trone family had leased a house. I would meet them and find out more about the work. It occurred to me then that I had never met an American before.

Mr. Trone showed us into the living room—he called it a "drawing room." When I asked him for more details about the work and the pay, he said: "We've got time for that. First you must explain something to me: How did fascism ever prevail in Germany? In Germany, of all places, the home of a great and powerful workers' movement." He had heard from our mutual acquaintances that Hans and I had been active antifascists in

Germany. "How could it have happened? How could you bear such a defeat? Can you explain that to me?" In his voice I again heard the personal reproach that I had already heard in Prague shortly after my escape from Germany. Trone spoke reasonably good German, but he seemed to get "Du" and "Sie" confused. I had to laugh, it was very amusing. This isn't the average American family, I told myself. We liked him and his wife, Florence, quite a lot, and we decided that I would take the job.

The Trones soon became our friends. I was often very tired in the evening; it was more than a little taxing to keep the house clean, cook for the family, and take care of little Alexandra, known to herself as Gugula. But we sat around in the living room, which the Trones continued to refer to as the "drawing room," listening to music and, more often than not, getting into an argument about the origins of fascism in Germany. Hans often came to visit. On Sundays we met at my parents' apartment in Butte Rouge. It was a chance for me to catch my breath. Until fall there would be enough time to find other work, and an apartment. Assuming that war did not break out in the meantime.

We were at my parents' apartment in Butte Rouge. And there were also a few friends from Paris who had dropped by for a visit. I had prepared a big bowl of grilled herring, just as we had always done in Berlin, and it was delicious. Herring tasted better than mackerel and was also cheaper. It was my birthday, August 23. In the midst of our celebration an announcement came over the radio: The Soviet Union and Germany have signed a nonaggression pact.

That just couldn't be! Talk of an agreement had been going around for some days, but it had to be lies, all lies. The Soviet Union? With fascist Germany?

"A pact between Stalin and Ribbentrop. Ridiculous!"

"So listen closely! Here—yes, the pact has been signed. Yes, the Soviet Union is making common cause with the Nazis. Do you believe it now?"

"Do we know what really took place? Can Russia stand by and watch while Hitler, with the help of France and England, prepares to attack the eastern front, finally leading to the destruction of the Soviet Union itself?"

"Can an alliance with fascism prevent it?"

"What else can be done? Who knows, who has an answer?"

Maybe our grandchildren will have a better understanding. . . .

# WAR!

That evening we were sitting in quiet and peaceful Marne-la-Coquette, in the Trones' "drawing room," listening to news on the radio. Gugula was still up and sat with us. We had not been able to get her to sleep; she must have sensed that something strange was in the air.

"The Wehrmacht has marched into Poland," said the voice on the radio. Then more news about the progress of the attack, and then, suddenly breaking in: "All American citizens are advised to leave France immediately and return to the United States."

I had leapt up, was standing in the middle of the room, peering first into one face and then another. Had the war begun? Now what?

Mr. Trone also stood up. "You will certainly want to go to your husband and your parents," he said to me. "Good, I'll drive you to Butte Rouge now."

"Yes, now. Yes, I'll get my things from upstairs. And what about you? Do you really have to ship out immediately?"

"We don't know ourselves . . . we'll see. Shall we go?"

Naturally, he and Florence had discussed what they would do in the event war broke out, he said, during the drive to Butte Rouge. They probably would have to leave France sometime in the next few days. Where to? Well, that was the big question. Maybe to one of the neutral countries in Europe. To Switzerland? Liechtenstein? Perhaps, as an American, he could be of some help to a few people who were now at risk in Europe; he had contacts with various relief agencies. I would, of course, hear from one of them soon.

Hans was already there with my parents when Trone and I arrived in Butte Rouge. My brother and Eva came upstairs with the baby. A few friends knocked on the door and joined us. We needed to be together, we emigrants. We all sat at the round table, drinking tea, keeping silent until it was time to talk. Now the war really was here, there was no going back . . . where was this going to lead? To a second world war? This time a

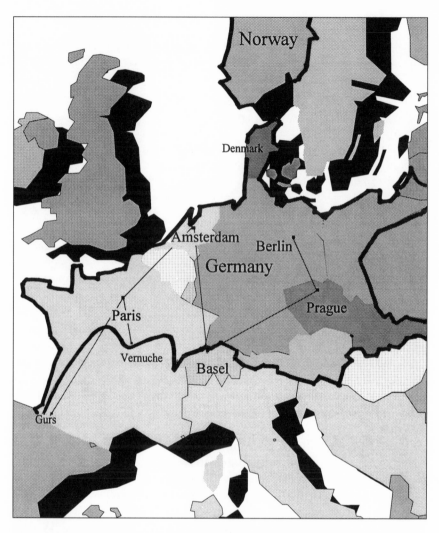

*By June of 1940, Hitler's armies controlled much of Europe. The French government classi-fied us as "enemy aliens" and we were both interned in French camps. I was sent to Gurs; Hans was sent to Vernuche.*

poison gas war, we knew. Where did we stand, we German emigrants? On the side of those who were fighting against fascism . . . on France's side, naturally. Against a national socialist Germany—unequivocally. But was it really that simple? Was it really that obvious? Is this really a war against fascism?

Against fascist Germany, yes. Six bloody years of terror, six years of untold sacrifices . . . but had this really brought the overthrow any closer? Would the internal opposition, the illegal Resistance, ever be able to liberate Germany?

So, would we ally ourselves with the imperialists?

It didn't matter, the Hitler regime was our enemy. We belonged to those who were fighting against Hitler. We had to join the fight.

There was no time for profound debate. No one could know how events would develop. Two days later, immediately following the declaration of war by France and England against Germany, the large red placards appeared on walls everywhere: enemy aliens, men up to the age of sixty-five years, were to report immediately to the Stade Colombe to be prepared for transport to *camps de concentration*. The "enemy aliens"— they were our men. Everyone who came from Germany and Austria: Jews, political emigrants, "citizens of the German Reich"—Nazis or not.

Hans my husband and Hans my brother packed their warmest things and, along with a group of other emigrants from Butte Rouge, took the bus into Paris. I, with a few other women, accompanied them to the bus stop along the highway; we were all quite confused. I heard one woman say, "How can they do this, just suddenly take our men away?" *"C'est la guerre, ma chérie,"* someone answered. Of us, my father was the only man who wouldn't have to go to the camp. He was over sixty-five.

Gas masks were distributed to the population. Everyone knew there would be poison gas in this war, and that it would affect civilians as well as soldiers. But we emigrants received no masks. People on the street had their masks attached to straps hanging around their necks, but we didn't have any masks. Not only would we be vulnerable to any gas attack, but the next day, when we went into Paris on the bus, everyone stared at us: we were obviously "enemy aliens"; we had no gas masks.

That evening we heard the first air-raid alarm. *"Alerte!"* The sirens howled, the citizens of Butte Rouge ran through the moonlit streets, along the rows of pink houses to the Abri, our communal air-raid shelter. The sirens continued to scream "Alarm," up high and down low. Eva ran in front of me carrying the one-year-old Catherine, who had already grown quite heavy. My father and I ran beside one another. Would his heart be able to take this—with his angina pectoris? I heard him gasping for breath. I can still hear him gasping, even today.

A wobbly flight of wooden stairs led down into the basement shelter. You couldn't see a thing, you only heard voices murmuring. Down there we waited for the bombs and the gas—but we emigrants didn't have masks. Several times we heard something that sounded like thunder in the distance. That's anti-aircraft artillery, someone said. We sat there for about two hours, and then the sirens howled again, this time a drawn-out wail, endless. No bombs, no gas attack—not this time. We went home through the dark streets. It was the first night in an endless series of nights in which we awakened in our darkened apartments and sprang out of our beds, fully clothed, to the sound of the sirens. On moonlit nights you could count on hearing the sirens, some nights two or three times. But no bombs fell.

The next day my friend Grete told me about the first night alert in Paris. For her building, for the entire quarter, the air-raid shelter was the nearest metro station. Masses streamed through the entrance, everyone carrying his gas mask, everyone except her and the other emigrants; she sensed the suspicious looks that followed her. Grete sat down in a stairway, wedged in among many others, and held a damp towel over her mouth and nose, as had been advised in the announcements. More and more people squeezed in, everyone becoming increasingly restless under the dark archways, they knew there would be poison gas . . . they could already smell it seeping in, despite the masks, which were apparently leaking. Some began throwing up, even Grete felt nauseated . . . yes, she certainly could smell gas . . . it was good to know that her child was in the countryside. Finally, after an eternity, the sirens howled an all-clear. But no, there had been no gas. No bombs either. Not yet.

There followed eight months of *drôle de guerre*, the phony war. Countless air-raid alarms without a single attack. The press continued to explain that every time a German bomber took off, all of France had to be put on *alerte*.

The very next day we had to find dark fabric to cover the windows. Everything was fair game, even clothing, the tablecloth, and dark-colored paper. But even when the windows were covered we were not allowed to turn on any lights. Once, in the beginning, we had apparently not been careful enough. It was late in the evening and we were sitting together in the ground-floor living room; a few neighbors were there, too. We spent a lot of time together these days; no one wanted to be alone in a darkened living room for very long. Suddenly we heard a loud knock; three men from the civil defense were standing in the dark outside our door. They had seen a tiny shaft of light shining through one of the windows and threatened stiff penalties if it should happen again.

How Paris had changed, the city of lights! Darkness everywhere. You could hardly tell where you were. I found my way along the rue Royale to the Madeleine—even it had been turned into a huge black clump in the gray night, not even a glimmer of its usual brilliant lights. The darkness was frightening, dreadful . . . but I had to get to the Pfemferts' apartment to see how Anja was getting on. I found her upset and disoriented. She was confused by the sirens, she said, and often didn't know whether they were signaling an alert or an all-clear, and she no longer went to the shelter, because some days ago she had gone down and found no one there. After sitting alone in the dark for over an hour, she learned that in her nervous state she had missed the alert and had taken shelter when the all-clear was sounded.

"That is all nonsense," she said, "but Franz. Franz Pfemfert, France's true old friend, friend of statesmen and writers, locked up in a French internment camp! As an enemy alien!" These are the words she repeated so often over the next half year.

Later, I also decided to stop going into the shelter at night. I had found office work in Paris and had to get up at six o'clock in the morning. We no longer had an apartment, so I slept on a mattress that we laid out on my parents' living-room floor. "Mother," I said, "I can't work during the day if I don't sleep at night. Don't wake me any more, I will certainly get used to sleeping through the sirens."

The men were held for about two weeks in the Stade Colombe, out in the wind and rain, without a roof over their heads. We women packed boxes of food and, most importantly, warm clothing for them. I can still see the endless lines of women standing in front of the stadium. Naturally, we were not allowed in and could not see our men, but we were told that we could leave packages at the front gate, and that they would be delivered to the addressees. Of course, we asked ourselves how it could be possible even to begin to try to make deliveries to these thousands of men, but we kept telling ourselves that one could never know, that we had to keep trying. We never found out what happened to the packages. All we knew was that the nourishment at the Stade Colombe consisted mainly of canned liver paté. Nothing but paté—even when you were very hungry, if you ever saw or smelled liver paté again in your life, it would make you sick. This is what the men later said when they talked about their stay in the Stade Colombe.

Then they were divided up and sent to various camps throughout the country. Hans, my husband, ended up in the Vernuche camp near Nevers; my brother Hans, in the Melay camp, where most of the Austrians had been imprisoned. There, to the melody of the Radetzky March, they composed verses describing the conditions in Melay. Their selection of words reflected their anger at being treated as "enemies" in the country where they had sought asylum: "Oh Melay, oh Melay, oh Me . . . kiss my . . . ."

Many of the men, Austrians as well as Germans, tried to enlist voluntarily in the French military. They were turned down, but would soon belong to a newly created category: *prestataires*. The definition of *prestataire* remained unclear throughout the course of the war; it could not be found in any dictionary. Perhaps it had something to do with the services they performed for the regular troops. Or with assistance. In any case, a *prestataire* did not have the same rights as a French soldier. It was also unclear what kind of uniform they would have, if they had any at all. "Now you see how France values your desire to be of service," said the ones who had decided against voluntary enlistment. The debate on the nature of the war continued among the political emigrants. The influential Communist party of France was against the war, this *drôle de guerre*. In their opinion it was simply another imperialist war.

The women, who had been left behind in Paris, began to form stronger and stronger bonds of friendship. We all felt a great need to stick together and support each other. I know that, at this time, I went home less often and started spending my weekday nights with friends in Paris. This was a great relief for me, because it meant that I didn't have to struggle with the now irregular bus service, and I saved a lot of time. At any rate, all I had in Butte Rouge was a mattress on the floor. My friends were happy when I stayed with them, because without our men the apartments had become so empty.

What was life like in exile, how do you survive—without work, without an income, without papers, when you have none of the things you are used to having in your own country? These are some of the questions Marlene, my youngest niece, recently began to ask me. It is difficult to remember exactly what it was like, I said, because you slowly lose your sense of what a normal life is. You try to carry on.

"No," said Marlene, "I don't understand what you mean. I want to know exactly what it's like when you have nothing, when you don't really belong anywhere. For example, what did you eat for lunch?"

"*Boudin*," I said, "blood sausage. *Boudin* is very cheap, you can fry it in oil, and it really tastes quite good, as long as you have some variety." "Okay, what did you eat for dinner?" Marlene asked. "Ground meat, they called it *bifteck tartar*, with lots of onions, and salt and pepper, sometimes with a raw egg on top . . . made from horse meat, of course. We Germans still have a silly prejudice against eating horse meat, but it really is delicious, and costs very little at the specialty butcher on the other side of the street, the shop with the golden horse head over the entrance." Marlene shuddered.

"And what do you wear? Where do you get clothes?" Marlene is thinking her way into our circumstances.

Yes, what about clothing? I am reminded of my friend Grete's gray velvet suit; it had become too small for her, so my mother altered it to fit me. I had two dresses, one green and one blue, which no longer fit because I had lost so much weight. So my mother altered them to fit Grete. Well, you see, this was the way you got along—and sometimes didn't get along.

Women knitted warm jackets and sweaters for their men. My mother taught me a crochet stitch; she called it a "Turkish stitch," if I remember correctly. It was easy to learn and went a lot faster than regular knitting. Once I had finished the gray-blue sweater, I decided, despite the ban, to go Vernuche and deliver it myself. It had turned out well and I was proud of my work. And I wanted to see Hans again.

Since the outbreak of war there were new regulations for emigrants, or maybe they applied to all foreigners. In any case, we needed special permission, a *sauf conduit*, whenever we wanted to leave our home region. However, in order to get a *sauf conduit* you needed a valid *carte d'identité*, and I didn't have one. Hans had gotten his while I was in the hospital. When I recovered and went to the prefecture, I was given a *refus de séjour*, meaning that my application for a residence permit had been refused, but not that I would be expelled. Why? There were never any explanations given.

The sweater was only one of the reasons that I felt such a need to visit Hans, in spite of the risks the journey entailed. I could have sent my good work by mail, but I had to see Hans and talk to him about the Foreign Legion; it was a very big worry. The men in the camps had been told that they had a decision to make about their futures. They were given a choice, either of volunteering for service in the Foreign Legion or of remaining in the concentration camps until the end of the war, *pour la durée de la guerre*. If a man decided to enlist in the Foreign Legion, he would not only be released immediately—to be sent directly to Africa, of course—but, instead of having to enlist for the normal five-year stint, he would *only* be required to serve until the end of the war, *pour la durée de la guerre*. And this wasn't all: volunteers were promised a *carte d'identité*, and in many cases a *carte de travail*, a work permit. After the war. But the generosity continued: anyone volunteering for service in the Foreign Legion would be allowed to marry!

The effect of this last regulation had been carefully calculated. One of the greatest problems for many young people during the emigration arose from the fact that they were not allowed to marry. To live together unmarried was not at all common in France at the time and often led to complaints from neighbors. Their children came into the world and were considered illegitimate before the law. Being able to marry, being *en ordre*, provided a glimmer of hope for many women who had suffered for years under the adversities of illegal companionship. Furthermore, women who were unmarried would receive no *allocation militaire*, no support for wives of soldiers. All of these considerations played an important role in the decision to enlist or not. And there was still the unanswered question: Where did we, the antifascist German emigrants, belong in the *drôle de guerre*?

The pressure the authorities put on the interned emigrants increased. They would not be released from the camps if they refused to enlist, no matter how long the war might last. And what would happen if the German army pushed on into the areas where the men were being held?

We wondered what motivated the French authorities to exert so much pressure on these men. Of course, the French Foreign Legion always needs men. And it was very expensive to feed thousands of interned, jobless men—and the government had no choice but to feed them. The solution: use the Foreign Legion to brush aside this painful problem with aliens one couldn't trust. The dream of building a Trans-Sahara Railway could finally be realized!

So, with no residence permit and no *sauf-conduit*, I left for Nevers. The journey went smoothly; my papers were not inspected. I had written Hans that I would be coming, but because everything was so unsure, I wasn't able to give him an exact date. As I walked down the street to the camp entrance, carrying my packages, I saw a group of prisoners standing behind the wire fence. They were apparently absorbed in a lively discussion.

And there was Hans! But the way they all looked—with stubbly beards, uncombed, thoroughly neglected. . . . Then they recognized me—a few of them recognized me—and, one after the other, they turned around and ran off. Hans reached his arms through the fence and took my hands in his. "Don't look at me now," he said, and put his hands over my eyes, "I'll be right back! I didn't know when you'd be coming—" and then he disappeared too.

He was the first to return, and the others soon followed—shaven, hair combed, reasonably clean. . . . But even the wild Legionnaires, a few of whom were in the camp, looked almost well-groomed. I had to laugh. How important it was to the men to look good! They always acted as if it made no difference to them at all.

Hans went into the kitchen with me, where he was allowed free entry. "I've become a cook," he reported proudly.

It was a short visit because I had to take the evening train back to Paris. His comrades were touchingly thoughtful and discreet, and we were able to spend the day together, undisturbed, in the kitchen.

We talked about the question of enlistment for a long time. I had been certain of it, we were both of the same opinion.

"You don't have to worry," said Hans. "I will never voluntarily enlist in the Foreign Legion, no matter how much pressure there is. I don't belong in the Sahara. Even if they actually keep us here until the end of the war, it's still better than the Legion. But maybe there's another way out." Then he added, as he so often did, "No need to hurry. . . ."

Our friends Erna and Rolf had also given the offer careful consideration. Like most of the others, they decided Rolf would enlist. They had a child, and everything would be so overwhelmingly difficult if Rolf were to remain in camp, and no one knew what was going to happen. . . . Now Africa might well be safer than Europe.

They had both fled to France in 1933, when they were still unmarried. Erna and I had been friends in Berlin and then had met again in Paris. When war broke out, Hans and Rolf ended up in the same camp, and over those several months I had often stayed with her in Paris, and she had often come to visit me with her little daughter.

Rolf enlisted and became a Legionnaire. They got married immediately after his enlistment. Erna's heart was heavy.

"Don't make so much of it," said Rolf, "I'll get a nice headstone; it will say: Died for *la carte d'identité.*"

This was Rolf's way of dealing with a difficult situation.

He got married while he was still in the camp but already in uniform. Everything was carefully prepared with the enthusiastic help of his comrades. The camp authorities gave their permission for a large wedding dinner to be held at a restaurant in the village. Under military surveillance, of course; and the guard was to be treated as a guest. Hans was best man, but his main role was to encourage the guard to drink so much that by the end of the dinner he could neither think clearly nor walk straight. Rolf's comrades had reserved a hotel room for the couple—of course, it was against regulations for the groom, who was a prisoner, to spend the night outside the camp. According to Hans's account, he kept refilling the guard's glass and then they toasted one another. *"A vôtre santé!"* said Hans, and the guard answered, getting jollier by the minute, *"A la vôtre!"* Near the end of the meal the guard's eyes fell shut. Then he almost fell off his chair and had to be carried back to the camp. Even Hans, I was told later, seemed somewhat sleepy at this point. People talked about the wedding for years.

# DRÔLE DE GUERRE

The new Legionnaires were granted a few days leave before they were to embark for Africa. You soon saw emigrants who had spent the months since the outbreak of war in concentration camps strolling through Paris. A few last days in Europe, and no one knew what was going to happen next. Many were now in uniform, walking arm in arm with their newly legitimized wives. Friends got together one more time before the journey to Africa.

These Legionnaires often found themselves in rather embarrassing situations. They had been issued their uniforms while they were still in camps and had gotten no training on how to behave like soldiers. These were people who had never served in the military before—how did one actually salute, whom was one required to greet, and how could one tell an officer's rank from his epaulets? The potential for error was great, and would certainly have been realized, had it not been for France's pronounced lack of military spirit and a good dose of Gallic humor.

Two friends on leave, Erich and Gustav, were walking along the boulevard Haussman—wandering through Paris one more time before everything broke loose. There were soldiers everywhere they turned. Gustav noticed that two men who were most certainly officers were approaching them; they might even be big mucketymucks, they looked like it. What to do in these circumstances, salute? In order to escape embarrassment, Gustav tried to get out of their way, as emigrant-Legionnaires were wont to do: he carefully scrutinized the other side of the boulevard; he didn't look at them. But they came up to him anyway, and one of them stopped in front of Gustav and said, *"Dis-donc, mon vieux—* say, buddy, what ranks do you suppose you are required to salute?"— smiled, saluted, and went on his way. "Man, Gustav," his friend Erich intoned in a nervous voice, "you can count your blessings, that was a general!"

Rudi was another one of the emigrant-Legionnaires on leave in Paris. He had just gotten out of the Vernuche camp, and when we met him in a bistro he said to me, "Maybe you don't know it yet, but Hans has enlisted."

I looked at him, astounded. "No, you're wrong, Hans has not enlisted," I said.

But Rudi stood his ground, Hans himself had told him as he was on his way to take his physical. Naturally, you had to pass the physical, but everyone knew that was just a formality, almost everyone was declared fit for service.

For a moment I was baffled. But, no, it had to be a mistake. Hans had not enlisted, he had promised me he never would. He would never ever go to Africa as a Legionnaire.

"You've got to see, there was nothing else we could do," said Rudi. "The pressure was too great." And the others tried to talk to me: I shouldn't get so upset, just keep calm, Hans wouldn't be alone, the emigrants would stick together. "And anyway," said a well-known author who considered himself quite a strategist, "if you think this through carefully, there are only two sides in this war. Can there be any doubt about which side we're on? Today, wherever the struggle against National Socialist Germany is being fought, that is where we belong. . . ."

That was the last straw. "Wherever? In the Foreign Legion?" I yelled at him. "And where's your place? Building the Trans-Sahara Railway? And who knows what's going to happen? The place of the German Left in the Sahara, to build the French their railway, because their own people haven't been able to take it? Because of hunger, epidemics, and overwork? That's supposed to be our place in the struggle against the Hitler regime?"

The next morning Hans was at home in Butte Rouge. My eyes opened wide in amazement. He wasn't in uniform.

"But you enlisted?"

"Yes, but only for a few hours."

"What's that supposed to mean?"

The medical commission had declared him unfit for service, he was *inapte*. Furthermore, he had been released from the camp for reasons of ill health; he was also unfit for captivity. Now he was back in Paris, released.

For reasons of ill health? What was wrong with his health?

"Everything's okay," said Hans. "As you know, a few of my friends in Vernuche are doctors. Old friends help each other out."

What exactly they had done, he didn't know. It didn't really make any difference; the important thing was, it worked. Accompanied by his friends, he had taken a rather roundabout way to his physical—as a volunteer he was allowed this degree of freedom—they took a stroll down a quiet path. His friends had brought something along that he was supposed to inhale. "Deeper, deeper!" they said.

Shortly after this, he was standing in front of the army physician and was again told to "Breathe deeply!" And he did. Very deeply, as his friends had instructed him.

"I thought I was hearing the blast of an organ," Hans reported. "The doctor shrank back. I had to steady myself. The doctor called in one colleague, and then another. I had to breathe for each of them; it was a frightening sound. After a short consultation they declared me unfit, both for the military and for imprisonment. The French military is required to pay a lifelong pension to anyone they sign up with bad lungs. That's why they're so careful about it."

From then on Hans was unfit for military service, but not unfit for labor. With the help of friends we were quickly able to find a very cheap hotel room in the center of Paris. The room was on the basement level and had a moldy smell. Dirt and dust from the street came in through the low window (one of those hinged windows that are called *vasistas*, in France; supposedly the term came from Prussian soldiers who, seeing such windows for the first time in 1870, asked, *Was ist das?*). This was the worst room we had ever had in Paris.

Hans was soon called into the work corps. He was to report to Chartres. After brief consideration, he decided not to follow this order. He didn't know the city, he didn't know anyone there, and he couldn't really speak French that well. He didn't even have a gas mask. All he had was an *accent boche*, a German accent.

"I can't afford to isolate myself with everything as uncertain as it is," he said. "I would have enjoyed seeing the cathedral, but we're not tourists now. I'm not going to Chartres."

Then he lay down on the narrow bed and promised me that he wouldn't get up. I called the office where he was registered and told them that he was unfortunately very ill and would not be able to go to Chartres. That same day, an official showed up in our basement room to check on Hans's health. Hans was alone at the time; he let the man in and then dragged himself, moaning, back to bed. He complained of unbearable back pain. The official said that he had also had that problem, he had hardly been able to take the pain, and where did it hurt? Yes, it was in exactly the same spot his own pain had been, and he massaged Hans's back, and Hans moaned even louder. The man from the work corps sat down on the edge of the bed. They talked for a while, and then got to telling stories about their families, how things had been at the end of the last war when they were children, and what was going to happen now, another world war? Then the visitor advised Hans to take it easy for now, not to lift anything, the pain would probably last another ten days or so; maybe hot compresses would help. When the pain was gone, Hans should report to him.

Life became more difficult for me too. Women who had no *carte d'identité* were to report to the prefecture every other day and then wait there until evening. Then we were called in to have our papers stamped: I got a stamp in my *refus de séjour*, my residence refusal.

War in Scandinavia. The air-raid alerts came more often now. We had to run down into the air-raid shelters again. Hans and I were walking somewhere in Paris and were surprised by an alarm. Into the cellar, the civil defense is chasing us off the streets! We are aliens, with no gas masks, there are no neighbors here who know us. We stand in a throng of people, squeezed up against one another, just no talking now, our *accent boche* will betray us as Germans. . . .

By evening we are in Butte Rouge. Alarm! My neighbor Sascha, whom I know from Berlin, is sitting next to me in the cellar. We hear bombs exploding. . . . That has to be Villacoublay, the nearby military airport, that's being attacked. With each explosion I sense Sascha's thin body shivering. . . . "It's only the anti-aircraft artillery," I whisper to her each time, and squeeze her hand. Don't know myself if it's true. But it calms her.

Hans was asked to write scripts for a Resistance station that broadcast to German troops from France. He went to work immediately. We were warned from all sides: Was this the right station? Was a party behind it? Which party? Or maybe even a branch of the French government? Where did the money come from? But Hans had no doubts. He had an opportunity to address German soldiers about the coming horror of the war, about the Terror. He knew how to talk to German soldiers. And it didn't matter to him who had made it possible. He no longer had to keep silent about the crimes of his country.

The announcer, Alex, was a young actor from the Rhineland. While he and Hans worked on the next broadcast, I went with his wife, Margit, to their apartment to get something to eat. I can remember, it was blood sausage. The doorbell rang, Margit opened the door, and two men stood in the hallway holding some kind of identification.

Might they come in? They had a few questions to ask. Might Monsieur be at home? No? well then, Madame would surely be able to help them. They had been sent by the Deuxième Bureau, you must know it, the secret police. No, I could certainly stay in the room.

"What does your husband do?" they asked Margit.

"He's an actor."

"And what is he doing now? Is he working?"

"He's an announcer for a French station that broadcasts to German troops. To the Germans."

"What kind of scripts does he broadcast?"

Margit looked at me furtively. I kept silent.

"He tells the Germans that the Führer is leading them into an evil war, into a fascist war, that Germany will surely lose this war, and this will bring suffering and horror to the country."

The men looked at one another.

"Defeatist propaganda, is that what you mean?"

Margit's eyes opened wide. Then she said: "Yes, defeatist, so that Germany will lose the war. . . ."

"Your husband is German?"

"Yes. A German who wants to keep his country from fighting a bloody war against the whole world."

"I see, he's like *le traître de Stuttgart* for us French. Your husband is a traitor to his own country."

Margit grew very pale.

"Where is this station located?"

"I have not been told."

Both men left without saying another word.

A few days later, when every German in France was again locked up in a stadium or a concentration camp, an exception was made for Alex. He was picked up at his apartment, arrested, and locked up in a Paris jail. Every morning and evening he was taken to the radio station under police surveillance. After his broadcast he was taken back to his cell. He didn't know who was writing the scripts.

For some time now my mother had been doing piecework at home: she sewed uniforms. She also took care of her grandchild, little Catherine, so that Eva could continue her work at the Paris Institute. But the incessant air-raid alerts made things impossible. Catherine was a sturdy child, she was heavy, and my mother had a bad heart. She took the child for walks, the sirens howled, the grandmother picked up her grandchild and ran with her to the communal shelter, carrying the child down the stairs . . . then, the only thing she knew was that she could not breathe, and only later, after the all-clear was sounded, did her neighbors from the rue Robert Hertz help her and the child back home. Eva would have to find someone else to take care of the child during the day.

The Germans overran Holland, Belgium, Luxembourg. The large red placards reappeared on walls everywhere. All men from Germany who for any reason had been released from camps over the winter were to turn themselves in. My brother, Hans, who had been sent back to Paris to continue work important to France's war effort, was picked up at home in the middle of the night and taken to Buffalo Stadium in Paris. Hans, my husband, was hauled out of our dirty basement room in Paris. They found each other among thousands of other emigrants at the stadium. After a few days they were transported to various camps in the western and southern regions of the country.

And red placards appeared again. This time women were also to be interned in *camps de concentration*, as they were called on the placards. The only exceptions were older emigrants and women with children.

This is how the *drôle de guerre* came to a close.

# PARIS AFTER JUNE 14

As soon as the afternoon of June 15, the day after the occupation of Paris, there was a knock on the door of my parents' apartment in Butte Rouge. They were upset; they hadn't slept. The previous day, when they saw that their neighbors from the rue Robert Hertz were fleeing, they threw a few of their possessions into the baby carriage and joined the procession, trying to keep up. More and more people joined in. After about two hours, the German troops had overtaken the refugees; they marched on, paying no attention to the fleeing mass of people. Many refugees turned around and went back to their homes. German troops set up camp in Butte Rouge. In spite of this, mother and father dragged themselves back home. Now they were alone in the apartment. My brother, my husband, and I had already been in internment for a number of months. Friends had taken Eva and the child to the station, where they were jostled back and forth by the chaotic crowds and had to push their way through the throngs of people onto an overcrowded train car.

When they heard a knock, my parents were terrified. Two German officers stood at the door. "Secret Police!" they said, and pushed the two aside.

"We are looking for Johannes Fittko, your son-in-law."

"He isn't here," my mother said.

"Where is he?"

"We don't know," said my father, "he doesn't live here."

There was an opened envelope on the table. One of the Gestapo officers grabbed it. "Who is this letter from?"

"From my niece, Mita, she lives in Brussels," said my mother. "We just got it and haven't had a chance to read it yet."

The officer glanced through the two pages of the letter and then put it in his briefcase.

"Where is your daughter?"

"She isn't here. We haven't heard anything from her for about a month."

"Where is your son-in-law living now?" The officer addressed my mother. He paged through his notebook. "Well, let's have it! Where is Johannes Fittko living?"

"He moved to Ivry," said my mother, and thought: but he is in a concentration camp.

"Don't lie to me! He does not live in Ivry!"

Later, my mother never could remember if she had consciously tried to mislead the man, or if in all her bewilderment she had simply made a mistake.

The officer looked at his notebook again.

"You're lying!" he shouted angrily. "Johannes Fittko does not live in Ivry, he lives in Issy! Is that right? Let's have the address!"

You know everything, my mother thought. Already, only one day after the occupation of Paris. "Maybe I misspoke," she said. "But I don't have his address."

They were not able to intimidate my parents. It was true that Hans had actually never given them the address of the hotel in Issy where he had registered, as a precaution, when the Germans began their advance into France.

Shortly after this the Gestapo summoned Hans's sister Marta in Berlin-Spandau to their headquarters. Their anger increased when they couldn't find him and were unable to get any information from her. "He was in Paris and has gotten away from us again!" the man shouted.

"Thank you, gentlemen," said Marta. "Now I know that my brother is still alive."

They let her leave.

My cousin Mita was arrested several days later in Brussels. When the Gestapo came she fled to the roof, but they found her there and took her away. After the war, one of the relief agencies received a report that she had been put on a train for Auschwitz. She never returned.

# AND THEN?

With the exception of the Legionnaires, who had been shipped off to North Africa, all emigrants, this time women included, were sent to French concentration camps. The activists among them, the best known political opponents of the national socialist dictatorship, were separated from the rest and locked up with criminals in the worst of the camps. They were designated *indésirables*, "undesirables." Among the women too, the political opponents of the Third Reich were considered especially dangerous and were segregated from the others—they were "undesirables."

What was going to happen? What would happen to us?

And, again and again, we asked ourselves and argued: Where do we belong? we, the German Left? Whose war is this? Is it a war against fascism? Or an imperialist war?

We asked ourselves: Can this be *the* war that will achieve the goals that we, despite all our sacrifices, despite all our suffering, could not achieve? Will it bring an end to national socialism?

We had to decide where we stood. We had to know what our role was, and what we could do.

For France, the decision was made: in less than five weeks, defeat; millions of Frenchmen fled the north. Masses of emigrants escaped from the concentration camps. Everyone streamed south because of the enemy invasion.

What happened to the thousands who, in part as Legionnaires, in part as refugees, landed in North Africa? They were also interned there, by the French government, in concentration camps.

Legionnaires were given a ten-day leave to go on vacation if they were able to produce a *certificat d'hébergement*, an invitation from a French family to stay in their home for that time. In Marseille, a lively market for the *certificats* immediately sprang up, and they were bought and sold at every possible price. Prostitutes, whose incomes were not particularly ample at the outbreak of war, were now able to supplement their earnings by making it possible for Foreign Legionnaires to come to the city on leave. The guests disappeared after a few days and tried to melt illegally into the crowds, as did all emigrants in France.

And then what?

France had been forced to surender. But did they have to sign the armistice with that clause—the treaty of shame—which offered the German emigrants up as a sacrifice to their former homeland? "Extradition on Demand" was the title of the paragraph in the treaty.

But we, we said, will not surrender. We have a task. It is our task to escape from this trap. We must save ourselves . . . we must try to save each other so that we can be alive and help to liberate Europe and the world from this barbarism.

And then?

What follows will not always progress smoothly. It lies in the hands of future generations.

# AFTERWORD

Shortly after its German publication in 1985, Lisa Fittko's first book, *Mein Weg über die Pyranäen* (Escape through the Pyrenees), was named Political Book of the Year. Then, in 1986, almost a half a century after a Nazi regime had taken away her citizenship, Lisa Fittko was awarded the Distinguished Service Medal, First Class, of the Federal Republic of Germany. She wrote the following letter of acceptance.

*October 21, 1986*

*Mr. Richard von Weizsäcker*
*President of the Federal Republic of Germany*
*Office of the President*
*Kaiser Friedrich Str. 16–18*
*5300 Bonn 1*

Dear Mr. President:

I am both moved and astonished at having been awarded the Distinguished Service Medal, First Class, of the Federal Republic of Germany. Forty-eight years ago, the National Socialist government rescinded my German citizenship because of "injurious activity and a lack of loyalty to the Reich." I shall keep the Distinguished Service Medal alongside that document I received so long ago. Both of them symbols of their time, separated by half a century.

When we, Hans Fittko and I, led antifascist refugees over the mountains, it was simply one way of carrying on the Resistance against Nazi barbarism. This unexpected award has touched me deeply as a sign of recognition for those who took part in the Resistance.

Yet my feelings of joy are mixed with a number of unsettling questions.

Are awards like this meant only for individuals? Shouldn't this be, first and foremost, an occasion for recognizing the Resistance movement as a whole? Young people always ask me: Why didn't anyone stand up against these crimes? It seems that the present generation knows little about the Resistance, that a significant part of the past has been neglected, and that this is an omission which needs redress. The true role of the Resistance is not yet a part of the German consciousness. Are we closing our eyes to this aspect of the past? Do people know how many Resistance groups there were? Where they worked? Do we know what they did? Are their words being passed along? Does anyone know how many people were executed? Do we know how many were shot "trying to escape"? Do we know how many were tortured to death?

The Resistance struggle against a criminal regime must be accorded its rightful place in our history, so that a new generation can believe in itself and in its future.

In the name of the German Resistance, I thank you for this award.

Respectfully yours,
*Lisa Fittko*

# JEWISH LIVES

LISA FITTKO
Solidarity and Treason: Resistance and Exile, 1933–1940

IDA FINK
A Scrap of Time

RICHARD GLAZAR
Trap with a Green Fence: Survival in Treblinka

ARNOŠT LUSTIG
Children of the Holocaust